1 AND 2 TIMOTHY AND TITUS

for

EVERYONE

20TH ANNIVERSARY EDITION WITH STUDY GUIDE

ENLARGED PRINT

NEW TESTAMENT FOR EVERYONE
20TH ANNIVERSARY EDITION WITH STUDY GUIDE
ENLARGED PRINT
N. T. Wright

Matthew for Everyone, Part 1
Matthew for Everyone, Part 2
Mark for Everyone
Luke for Everyone
John for Everyone, Part 1
John for Everyone, Part 2
Acts for Everyone, Part 1
Acts for Everyone, Part 2
Romans for Everyone, Part 1
Romans for Everyone, Part 2
1 Corinthians for Everyone
2 Corinthians for Everyone
Galatians and Thessalonians for Everyone
Ephesians, Philippians, Colossians and Philemon for Everyone
1 and 2 Timothy and Titus for Everyone
Hebrews for Everyone
James, Peter, John and Judah for Everyone
Revelation for Everyone

1 AND 2 TIMOTHY AND TITUS

for

EVERYONE

20TH ANNIVERSARY EDITION WITH STUDY GUIDE

ENLARGED PRINT

N. T. WRIGHT

STUDY GUIDE BY MICHAEL L. KIRKINDOLL

WESTMINSTER
JOHN KNOX PRESS
LOUISVILLE • KENTUCKY

© 2003, 2004, 2023 Nicholas Thomas Wright
Study guide © 2023 Westminster John Knox Press

First published in Great Britain in 2003 by the
Society for Promoting Christian Knowledge
36 Causton Street
London SW1P 4ST
www.spckpublishing.co.uk

Copublished in 2004 by the Society for Promoting
Christian Knowledge, London, and Westminster John Knox Press,
100 Witherspoon Street, Louisville, KY 40202.

20th Anniversary Edition with Study Guide
Enlarged Print
Published in 2023
by Westminster John Knox Press
Louisville, Kentucky

23 24 25 26 27 28 29 30 31 32—10 9 8 7 6 5 4 3 2 1

Cover design by Allison Taylor

Library of Congress Cataloging-in-Publication Data is on file at the Library of Congress, Washington, DC.

ISBN-13: 978-0-664-26650-9 (U.S. edition)
ISBN-13: 978-0-664-26880-0 (U.S. enlarged print)

Most Westminster John Knox Press books are available at special quantity discounts when purchased in bulk by corporations, organizations, and special-interest groups. For more information, please e-mail SpecialSales@wjkbooks.com.

For
the Diocese of Durham
a small gift from its chief pastor

CONTENTS

CONTENTS

2 TIMOTHY

TITUS

INTRODUCTION TO THE
ANNIVERSARY EDITION

It took me ten years, but I'm glad I did it. Writing a guide to the books of the New Testament felt at times like trying to climb all the Scottish mountains in quick succession. But the views from the tops were amazing, and discovering new pathways up and down was very rewarding as well. The real reward, though, has come in the messages I've received from around the world, telling me that the books have been helpful and encouraging, opening up new and unexpected vistas.

Perhaps I should say that this series wasn't designed to help with sermon preparation, though many preachers have confessed to me that they've used it that way. The books were meant, as their title suggests, for everyone, particularly for people who would never dream of picking up an academic commentary but who nevertheless want to dig a little deeper.

The New Testament seems intended to provoke all readers, at whatever stage, to fresh thought, understanding and practice. For that, we all need explanation, advice and encouragement. I'm glad these books seem to have had that effect, and I'm delighted that they are now available with study guides in these new editions.

N. T. Wright
2022

INTRODUCTION

On the very first occasion when someone stood up in public to tell people about Jesus, he made it very clear: this message is for *everyone*.

It was a great day – sometimes called the birthday of the church. The great wind of God's spirit had swept through Jesus' followers and filled them with a new joy and a sense of God's presence and power. Their leader, Peter, who only a few weeks before had been crying like a baby because he'd lied and cursed and denied even knowing Jesus, found himself on his feet explaining to a huge crowd that something had happened which had changed the world for ever. What God had done for him, Peter, he was beginning to do for the whole world: new life, forgiveness, new hope and power were opening up like spring flowers after a long winter. A new age had begun in which the living God was going to do new things in the world – beginning then and there with the individuals who were listening to him. 'This promise is for *you*,' he said, 'and for your children, and for everyone who is far away' (Acts 2.39). It wasn't just for the person standing next to you. It was for everyone.

Within a remarkably short time this came true to such an extent that the young movement spread throughout much of the known world. And one way in which the *everyone* promise worked out was through the writings of the early Christian leaders. These short works – mostly letters and stories about Jesus – were widely circulated and eagerly read. They were never intended for either a religious or intellectual elite. From the very beginning they were meant for everyone.

That is as true today as it was then. Of course, it matters that some people give time and care to the historical evidence, the meaning of the original words (the early Christians wrote in Greek), and the exact and particular force of what different writers were saying about God, Jesus, the world and themselves. This series is based quite closely on that sort of work. But the point of it all is that the message can get out to everyone, especially to people who wouldn't normally read a book with footnotes and Greek words in it. That's the sort of person for whom these books are written. And that's why there's a glossary, in the back, of the key words that you can't really get along without, with a simple description of what they mean. Whenever you see a word in **bold type** in the text, you can go to the back and remind yourself what's going on.

There are of course many translations of the New Testament available today. The one I offer here is designed for the same kind of reader: one who mightn't necessarily understand the more formal, sometimes even ponderous, tones of some of the standard ones. I have tried, naturally, to keep as close to the original as I can. But my main aim has been to be sure that the words can speak not just to some people, but to everyone.

Let me add a note about the translation the reader will find here of the Greek word *Christos*. Most translations simply say 'Christ', but most modern English speakers assume that that word is simply a proper name (as though 'Jesus' were Jesus 'Christian' name and 'Christ' were his 'surname'). For all sorts of reasons, I disagree; so I have experimented not only with 'Messiah' (which is what the word literally means) but sometimes, too, with 'King'.

Unlike the rest of Paul's letters, which (except for Philemon) are addressed to whole churches, the 'Pastoral Letters' are addressed to individuals: two to Timothy, whom we know from Acts and from several other references in Paul, and one to Titus, about whom Paul speaks warmly elsewhere in his writings. These letters are very practical, offering encouragement and advice on the day-to-day life of a local church and the role of the chief pastor within it. At the same time, they constantly give us glimpses of a rich theological picture of Jesus, and of the power of the gospel. Many have wondered whether Paul himself could have written these letters, which are very different in some respects from the others. This book isn't the place to discuss such matters; what concerns us here is what the letters say and how they relate to us today. So here it is: 1 and 2 Timothy and Titus for everyone!

Tom Wright

1 TIMOTHY

1 TIMOTHY 1.1–7

True Teaching about the Truth

[1]Paul, an apostle of Messiah Jesus according to the command of God our saviour and Messiah Jesus our hope, [2]to Timothy, my true child in faith: grace, mercy and peace from God the father and Messiah Jesus our Lord.

[3]This is my charge to you, just as it was when I went to Macedonia: stay in Ephesus, so that you can tell the relevant people not to teach anything different, [4]or to cling on to myths and endless genealogies. That sort of thing breeds disputes rather than the instruction in faith that comes from God. [5] The goal of such instruction is love – the love that comes from a pure heart, a good conscience and sincere faith. [6]Some people have wandered off from these things and turned aside to foolish talk. [7]They want to be teachers of the law; but they don't understand either what they're talking about or the things about which they pronounce so confidently.

I remember with considerable embarrassment one of the very first sermons I ever preached.

In my mind's eye I could see it so well. I knew – or thought I knew – what I wanted to say. But when I sat down to put it together, to write it out and see how it would go, it all somehow ran away from me. I remember going to one of the biblical passages that was to be read in the service and discovering to my horror that, on closer inspection, it was a lot more complicated than I had thought when I had first glanced at it. I remember trying to work in all sorts of points that I'd only just come across, and had not really thought through. And I remember my mind and imagination jumping to and fro between the mental image I had of what a great preacher ought to sound like, the texts in front of me on the desk, and the ideas, jottings and illustrations in my notebook.

Fortunately, I don't have a clear memory of how the sermon went on the day. I suspect there is a good reason for that. By the time I stood up in the pulpit, I no longer knew what the sermon was aiming at. I knew plenty of things I wanted to say, and plenty that I thought the congregation needed to hear, but I couldn't have told you then, and I can't tell you now, what I wanted the sermon to *achieve*. I was in the state described in the classic story of the seminarian submitting a draft sermon to the college principal. He sat anxiously while the great man read it through.

'Will it do?' asked the student.

'Do what?' replied the principal.

So when I read what Paul is saying to Timothy about different types of teaching, I know from the inside, as it were, at least part of what he's guarding against. He has in mind two basic types of teaching. One goes round and round in circles, picking up interesting ideas and theories and playing with them endlessly – though not necessarily having a very detailed understanding of what such things might really be all about. The other has a clear aim, cuts out anything that gets in the way of it, and goes straight to the point.

A good deal in this letter, and in 2 Timothy and Titus as well, is concerned with these two types of teaching, and we shall see Paul come back to the point from several different angles. The three letters, taken together, are usually called 'the Pastoral Letters', partly because Paul is acting as a pastor to Timothy and Titus, and partly because he is writing to instruct them in their own pastoral ministries and in the ministries that they are to establish in their various congregations. But they might equally well be called 'the Teacher's Manual', because so much of what they contain is about the kind of teaching that Christian leaders should be giving – and, just as much, the kind they shouldn't.

Before we go any further, though, are we really sure these letters were written by Paul himself? Everybody in the early church seems to have taken it for granted that they were. But in the last two hundred years many writers have pointed out several ways in which the letters sound and feel significantly different to the main letters (Romans, Galatians and so on) which we know to have come from Paul himself. Some now regard the question as settled: Paul, they say, couldn't possibly have written them. Others see it as still open. Some still insist that they must have been written by Paul. There are, after all, some very personal details which it would be strange for anyone else to have made up.

It's a complicated matter, and this kind of book isn't the place to go into it in any detail. But we do need to remind ourselves that when these letters were written – that is, some time between about 50 and 100 AD – it was quite common for someone to write in someone else's name. This didn't necessarily mean they were (as we would say now) committing forgery. They might be genuinely following through the thought of the person whose name they were using, and applying it to a new situation. I don't think this is a full explanation of the facts in this case, but it's worth bearing in mind.

Equally, we should remember that Paul himself is an example, even in the letters everybody agrees really do come from him, of how the same person can write in very different styles from one situation to another. A good example is his two letters to Corinth. They are so different in style and tone that if they were the only pieces of his work we possessed we might well imagine that he could only have written one of them, and that someone else must have written the other. But it's certain that he wrote both. The difference between the Paul of Romans and the Paul of the Pastorals is not much greater than the difference between the Paul of 1 Corinthians and the Paul of 2 Corinthians. For the purposes of this book I'm going to leave the question open, but will continue referring to the author as 'Paul' for the sake of ease.

One of the things we can be quite sure of is that the 'Paul' of these letters is every bit as keen on teaching the truth as the 'Paul' of Romans and the rest. And we have here a crisp, clear statement of what that teaching aims at: not just the conveying of information, but a whole way of life, summed up in verse 5 under three headings: genuine love, good conscience and sincere **faith**.

Underneath these we can detect two concerns which run through these letters. First, Paul is anxious that everyone who professes Christian faith should allow the **gospel** to transform the whole of their lives, so that the outward signs of the faith express a living reality that comes from the deepest parts of the personality. Second, he is also anxious that each Christian, and especially every teacher of the faith, should know how to build up the community in mutual love and support, rather than by the wrong sort of teaching or behaviour, tearing it apart. We know even today, with two thousand years of history, how easily things can seem to fall apart. How much more fragile must the little churches have seemed in those early days, with tiny communities facing huge problems.

But, as the opening greeting insists, they do not face those problems alone. Paul's **apostle**ship is rooted in God's command to him, and he assures Timothy of God's grace, mercy and peace. The God he invokes is the 'saviour' – a title often used in the first century for the Roman emperor, the Caesar of the day; and the Jesus he follows as his hope is the King, the **Messiah**, the world's true Lord. Once we get that straight, there should be no need for teachers to go round and round in circles, fussing about strange old stories or 'endless genealogies', as some of the Jewish teachers of the day seem to have done. There is no point, either (verses 6 and 7), in people trying to teach the Jewish **law** to Christian congregations without really understanding, as Paul certainly did, what it actually is and how it would need to be applied. No: the teaching of the gospel itself, and of the way of life which flows from it, must not be a muddled, rambling thing, going this way and that over all kinds of complex issues. It must go straight to the point and make it clearly, so that the young Christians who so badly need building up in their faith may learn the deep, rich, basic elements because of which genuine Christianity stands out from the

5

world around it, rather than hiding its life inside a thick outer casing of complex and impenetrable ideas.

1 TIMOTHY 1.8–11

The Purpose of the Law

> [8]We know, after all, that the law is good – if someone uses it lawfully! [9]We recognize that the law is not laid down for people who are in the right, but for the lawless and disobedient, for the godless and sinners, the unholy and worldly, for people who kill their father or mother, for murderers, [10]fornicators, practising homosexuals, slave traders, liars, perjurers, and those who practise any other behaviour contrary to healthy teaching, [11]in accordance with the gospel of the glory of God the blessed one that was entrusted to me.

We stood by the stream, looking across to the other side of the valley. It was a perfect spring day: gentle breeze, high cloud, bright sunshine, the hills around us at their best. Somewhere in the distance we could hear a sheep calling to its lamb.

'We've never been across there', said my companion. 'All the times we've walked up here, not once have we taken the southern route and seen the view from those hills.'

He knew as well as I did why we hadn't been that way. We got the map out once more and looked at it. A mile or so to the south of us there were small block capitals in red ink. DANGER AREA, it said. The message was repeated every half mile or so. Some way to the south there was an army camp. The whole area was used as a practice ground for military manoeuvres. The frustrating thing that day was that we'd been up in the hills for hours and hadn't heard any gunfire. The chances were that the soldiers had other things to do just then. We could probably have walked across the whole terrain and been completely safe. But when the map says DANGER there is really no sense in even thinking about it. We looked wistfully at the unexplored hills, and set off north for one of our old familiar walks.

Now imagine for a moment that you had a map which *only* marked danger. Supposing the only words on the whole area covered by the map were signs, not only of army firing ranges, but of sheer cliffs you might fall off, dangerous intersections where road accidents might occur, bridges that looked safe but might collapse if you tried to cross them, and so on. Suppose there were no other words or symbols – nothing to tell you the name of the towns and villages, no signs of where there were good views, picnic spots, pretty paths beside the rivers, places where you could get a meal or a drink or a bed for the night. It would be a depressing sort of map, wouldn't it? It might make you want to stay at home and never venture out of doors. It reminds me of that teasing line in Proverbs (26.13): when someone says 'There is a lion in the streets!', they may be telling the truth, but they may simply be looking for an excuse not to go to work that day.

The main point of the present passage is that the Jewish **law** is like a map which only marks danger. Paul, having left Timothy in charge of the church in Ephesus, was aware that there were some teachers there who were very keen on the Jewish law. It was regarded, after all, as the basis not only of personal morality but of the whole Jewish way of life. Perhaps, as he suggests in the previous passage, some of the Jewish Christians in Ephesus were making the law central to their development of Christian teaching. And that, he says, is like sending people off for a walk in the country when all that the map tells them is where they should *not* go.

For such a purpose, he says, the law is very useful. That, in fact, is what it's there for; using it like that is the appropriate thing to do, the 'lawful' way of handling it (verse 8). If you want to know what not to do, the Jewish law will give you an outline, marking several types of attitude and behaviour with the word DANGER, or perhaps 'No Road This Way'. It won't tell you what you *should* do; by itself, it won't encourage you to think through and live out the attractive, outgoing life of love and service which was, for Paul, what being a Christian was all about. So, somewhat contemptuously we may feel, he lists the people for whom the teaching of the law ought to be useful: people who are always wandering off into danger areas, who seem bent on going too near the edge of moral cliffs or trying to cross bridges that will crumble underneath them and send them crashing into the river below. The implication throughout is: well, if they want to teach the law, that's fine, but it presumes that their hearers are people of this sort – whereas, if they are working in a Christian community, their hearers ought *not* to be people of that sort!

He clearly has in mind not just the Jewish law in the sense of the first five books of the Bible (that's one meaning 'the law' could have at the time), but more specifically the Ten Commandments which we find in Exodus 20.1–17. We mightn't have noticed this with the first words in the list in verses 9 and 10 – lawless, disobedient, godless, sinners, unholy, worldly – but it becomes clear in what follows. The fifth commandment deals with the respect due to parents, the sixth with murder, the seventh with adultery, the eighth with stealing, the ninth with giving false evidence, and the tenth – often regarded as a kind of catch-all at the end of the list – with covetousness. From near the end of verse 9 and through verse 10 Paul seems to have these six commandments in mind, and is expanding their range a bit: the extreme opposite of honouring parents is killing them, the commandment against adultery should be taken to include all kinds of non-married sexual activity, the most dramatic example of stealing is when you steal an actual human being to sell as a slave. Paul, too, adds a catch-all at the end of his list: 'any other behaviour which is against healthy teaching'. The fact that he's following the commandments quite closely here implies that we should see those earlier terms, beginning with 'lawless', as a way of describing people who break the first three commandments at least – putting God first, not making idols, not taking God's name in vain. (The fourth commandment, about keeping the **sabbath**, was controversial in early Christianity, as Romans 14 makes clear; but that's a topic for another occasion.)

The point of it all seems to be, not so much to list various types of bad behaviour for their own sake, but to say: the law is fine, if you want a map of where all the dangers lie. There are indeed dangerous types of behaviour out there, and the **gospel** message of Jesus, through which God's glory is truly revealed (verse 11), is just as much opposed to them as the Jewish law is. But don't imagine that by teaching the Jewish law you will do more than put up some more signposts warning people about these dangers. What's far more important is to explore the gospel itself, the message which was entrusted to Paul and the other **apostles**. When the law was given in the first place, God also revealed his glory to Moses (Exodus 32—34), despite the fact that the people had already broken the law. Here, as in 2 Corinthians 3 and 4, Paul declares that, however good the law is, it is the gospel, not the law, which reveals God's glory.

1 TIMOTHY 1.12–17

Paul as an Example of God's Saving Grace

> [12]I thank Messiah Jesus our Lord, who gave me strength. He regarded me as trustworthy by appointing me to his service – [13]even though I used to say blasphemous things against him, and persecuted his people violently! But I received mercy, because in my unbelief I didn't know what I was doing. [14]And the grace of our Lord was more than enough for me, with the faith and love that are in Messiah Jesus. [15]Here is a word you can trust, which deserves total approval: 'Messiah Jesus came into the world to save sinners' – and I'm the worst of them! [16]But this was why I received mercy: so that in me, precisely as the worst, Messiah Jesus could demonstrate the full scale of his patience, and make me a pattern for those who were going to believe

in him and so attain the life of the age to come. [17]To the King of the ages, the one and only God, immortal and invisible, be honour and glory to the ages of ages, Amen!

When I was a boy, television was in its infancy. There was only one channel, and there wasn't very much to watch on it. But, when I graduated off the programmes for little children (*Andy Pandy* and *Bill and Ben, the Flowerpot Men*), there was one regular serial that stands out in my mind: *The Lone Ranger*. I didn't know then what I know now, that the story of the one Texas Ranger left alive after the death of colleagues and family fitted into a pattern of American stories which were shaped by, and then shaped in turn, the way many Americans saw the world. Like a lot of young boys, I was excited by the exploits of this quiet, understated hero.

The Lone Ranger's horse, Silver, became almost as famous as the man himself. Silver shared his master's exploits, and seemed to understand exactly what he was doing and where he needed help. But when we first meet Silver, at the start of the long and almost epic cycle of Lone Ranger stories, the horse is not only unbroken, untamed, but is assumed to be unbreakable, untameable. Tonto, the Native American who becomes the Lone Ranger's close friend and ally, declares that it's impossible to tame a horse like that. There is an utter wildness and wilfulness about him which would make normal horse-tamers give up and try their skills on easier animals. But the Lone Ranger is not to be put off. This is the horse for him. By some secret means he calls the animal to be his, and the horse responds and gives him a lifetime of service.

Now there are other interesting themes here as well, notably the biblical one of the truly human being who is put in charge of the animals (see Genesis 2.19–20). But the point I want to make is this: from the moment when the Lone Ranger shows that he can tame the untameable horse and make it into his servant, and even in a measure his friend, the viewer knows that he will be able to conquer all other obstacles in his path as well. He has already taken the hardest case, and the easy ones will now be – well, easy. And that is precisely the point Paul is making when he talks of what God had done in his life. God has taken the wildest, most violent of blaspheming persecutors, and has transformed him into not only a believer but also a trusted **apostle** and evangelist. If God can do that, there is nobody out there, no heart so hard, no anger so bitter, that it remains outside the reach of God's patient mercy.

This is the point of verses 15 and 16, which form the centre of this passage. Paul had been the worst sinner; the word for 'worst' literally means 'first' or 'chief'. 'Chief Sinner' – that, looking back, is how Paul sees his former life! Not that it had seemed like that at the time, of course; he had thought he was doing God's will. Sincerity is clearly not enough. Now he realizes that his angry words against the early Christians had been blasphemous, slandering the people who were following King Jesus, and that the angry deeds that had gone with them were just like the persecutions that God's people had always had to endure. He was doing to God's true people what the wicked pagans had done to Israel in times past. The fact that he thought he was defending Israel against heresy only made it worse. This is the sort of man he had been. The Christians, doing their best to hide from his violent attacks, would surely have regarded him as way beyond the scope of God's mercy.

But nobody is beyond that loving reach. Paul adds an interesting note, similar to what he says about his fellow Jews in Romans 10.2–3: he was acting 'ignorantly, in unbelief'. Just as Jesus had prayed that God would forgive the Roman soldiers who were nailing him to the cross, because they didn't know what they were doing (Luke 23.34), so Paul looks back and sees that he had had no idea what he was really doing. No doubt he would say the same about others in his condition. And God loves to show to just such people how patient and forbearing he really is (verse 16). Paul thus becomes a pattern, a model, for the way in which God reveals his love to the most unlikely people and brings them to **faith**. And, as always in Paul, faith in turn becomes the key to membership in 'the **age to come**', the new age for which the Jews had longed. Paul had originally supposed that the blasphemous nonsense of the Christian message might hold back the day when God's new age would dawn for Israel and the world. Now he sees that the message is actually about this new age, dawning in Jesus and now spreading its light to all the nations.

Paul has become one of the central agents of this spreading light. He finds new strength bubbling up inside him for the tasks to which God has called him, and he knows this comes from King Jesus himself (verse 12). What's more, he knows that this is a sign that God is considering him trustworthy. In a world of suspicion, of lies and counter-lies, God's project to save the world is built on trust. This seems intolerably risky: surely God isn't going to trust frail, fallible mortals? But that, too, is part of God's strange way, the way of love. And it's because of that initial trust that Paul can in turn trust others to help him in his work. That's one part of what the Pastoral Letters are all about.

As so often, the passage which seemed to be all about Paul is in reality all about God and his grace and love. So it's quite appropriate that Paul ends it with an outburst of praise to the one true God (verse 17). This is the line made famous in the great hymn of Walter Chalmers Smith (1824–1908), 'Immortal, invisible, God only wise'. When your train of thought brings you back to praise this one and only God, you know he is trusting you and equipping you for his service. That is one of the reasons why worship is central to all genuine Christian living.

1 TIMOTHY 1.18–20

The Battle of Faith

> [18]I am giving you this command, Timothy my child, in accordance with the prophecies which were made about you before, so that, as they said, you may fight the glorious battle, [19]holding on to faith and a good conscience. Some have rejected conscience, and their faith has been shipwrecked. [20]I include Hymenaeus and Alexander in that category. Indeed, I have handed them over to the satan, so that they may be taught not to blaspheme.

In the days before ships could navigate by satellite, the compass was the most crucial item on board. Whether it was sunny or snowing, whether it was day or night, whether the ship was on course or off course, the compass was the vital sign that told the sailors which direction they were going. There were other problems, of course – a cloudy night would mean no stars, and no stars meant that they wouldn't know how far north or south they were – but the compass remained at the heart of the ship's operation.

So if the compass got dirty, or stuck, or pulled out of its true line by some strong magnetic force, the ship was in real trouble. Imagine being blown about in a small boat in the middle of the ocean, without the slightest idea which way you were facing. It's enough to make you panic just to think about it.

For many serious-minded writers in the ancient world, the human equivalent to the compass was the conscience. The strange, mysterious little voice that tells you what's right and what's wrong, sometimes whispering, sometimes shouting, seldom totally silent – many thinkers, both Jewish and pagan, saw it as a kind of divine presence, to guide and warn the human race. Of course, not all societies agree on the exact detail of their various moral codes. But almost all have the same basic ethical beliefs (the wrongness of murder, theft and so on). The conscience can, as it were, be educated this way or that. But it's still there, the voice that says 'Yes, this is right', or 'No, you shouldn't do that'.

What we find in Paul is the beginning of a Christian view of conscience. Paul would have agreed with the moral teachers of his day on the importance of conscience, and would have said that the reason it was there was that the one God, the creator, had implanted it in the human heart as a small but significant witness to the way he wanted humans to live. But, since Paul was quite clear that nobody could in fact live the way God wanted by their own unaided efforts, he would also have stressed that to be properly obedient to the true promptings of conscience, one would have to come to **faith**, accepting the gift of new **life** from God in the power of the **spirit**. That way, one would become a truly human being at last, able to reflect the image of the creator God. The pagan moral teachers could point the way, but they couldn't actually help people to do what they knew they should. Seneca, one of the greatest moral teachers of Paul's day, was himself criticized for failing to live up to the standards he taught to others. He admitted it.

But what if you stopped listening to your conscience altogether? That is what Paul says some people have begun to do. He doesn't explain why they would think this appropriate; but of the two names he mentions, Hymenaeus and Alexander, one of them, Hymenaeus, crops up again in 2 Timothy 2.17. There Paul says that he and another man are teaching that 'the **resurrection** has already happened', in other words, that Christians are already fully 'raised from the dead' in all the senses that matter, and have therefore presumably passed beyond the need to make the effort to obey the normal moral codes. This has, in fact, been a familiar feature of some types of would-be Christian piety: when people discover what a dramatic difference God's power can make in their lives, they sometimes imagine that they have been set free from all ordinary constraints, and have therefore put their consciences into a back room and locked the door. Not surprisingly, this has often led to moral and spiritual disaster, as people then give free rein to all kinds of impulses over which conscience would normally provide a control.

Paul's reaction in such cases is swift and strict: he has 'handed them over to **the satan**', to teach them not to say and do wicked things. As in 1 Corinthians 5, this seems to mean that such people are to be put out of the Christian assembly, forbidden to meet with, and eat with, the rest of the church. Paul saw the fellowship of the church as the place above all where the power of God was active to heal, guide, lead and direct individual Christians. To forbid people access to it was therefore tantamount to sending them away into outer darkness, to a place where the only spiritual influence they might come under would be that of 'the **accuser**', the satan. The aim, of course, is that after a very short time in such a condition they would realize their mistake and come back with sorrow and penitence, ready to learn wisdom. That is what probably happened in the other case, as 2 Corinthians 2 seems to indicate.

Paul's charge to Timothy is, of course, that he shouldn't go the same route as Hymenaeus and Alexander, but that he should hold on tight to two things: faith and a good conscience. Faith reaches out and grasps the God who made you and is remaking you through Jesus and the spirit. Conscience, educated now by the same spirit according to the pattern and teaching of Jesus, steers you through the choppy and dangerous waters of life. In pastoral work what you often need is a rule of thumb, a quick and easily memorable summary of certain basic points which could in principle be developed at more length but which a busy person needs to recall without difficulty. 'Fight the glorious battle, holding on to faith and a good conscience.' Simple, clear and challenging.

1 TIMOTHY 2.1–7

The First Rule: Prayer for the World

¹So, then, this is my very first command: God's people should make petitions, prayers, intercessions and thanksgivings on behalf of all people – ²on behalf of kings, and all who hold high office, so that we may lead a tranquil and peaceful life, in all godliness and holiness. ³This is good; it is acceptable with God our saviour, ⁴who wants all people to be saved and to come to know the truth. ⁵For, you see,

> There is one God,
> and also one mediator between God and humans,
> Messiah Jesus, himself a human being.
> ⁶He gave himself as a ransom for all,
> and this was testified when the time was right.

⁷This is why I was appointed a herald and an apostle (I'm speaking the truth, I'm not lying!), a teacher of the Gentiles in faith and truth.

When did you last make a list of people you wanted to pray for? Whose were the first names you wrote down?

Most of us would start with the people we know and love best: our spouse, our children, our parents; other close relatives; friends we see frequently, who are uppermost in our minds; people facing illness or death. Prayer lists often go out in concentric circles, with ourselves in the middle – and we will be sure, no doubt, to pray for all the various concerns that hammer away at us in our own lives, our work, our responsibilities, our worries.

Paul prays for his friends and relatives, of course; we know that from things he says over and over again. But in this passage he strongly urges that we should start, as it were, at the other end. We should pray for the people who hold the world together by their rule, leadership and authority.

For many Christians today, particularly those who (like me) have grown up in the Western world and have never known war or major civil disturbance in our own country, this often seems quite remote. We are happy (more or less) with our democratic institutions, our systems of government. We vote every few years, we answer opinion polls from time to time, and we have a sense that we live in a free society. We're not particularly eager to swap it for another system. Yes, we'd like our politicians to use our tax money more effectively, we grumble about some of their policies, but what they do doesn't drive us to our knees to pray for them, to beseech God to guide them and lead them to create a better world for us all to live in. Many Christians who are reasonably content with their country are tempted to think that praying for kings and governments is a rather boring, conformist thing to do. It looks like propping up the status quo.

But supposing you live (as many readers of this book will do) in countries which have had unstable government, perhaps tyranny, for many years. Supposing you live with the dread of the knock on the door after dark which means that the secret police have come to take someone away, perhaps to be tortured or killed. Supposing 'the government' knows about this, plays along with it, or is even directly responsible. Wouldn't you be praying night and day for good, strong, wise, just rulers who would hold your world together and prevent the bullies and the cynical power-seekers from having it all their own way?

And, since we now live in such a small world, where messages, pictures and sounds can flash around the world in a matter of seconds, where the pain of someone in the Sudan can appear instantly on screens in America or New Zealand, should we not all be joining together and praying for good government on a worldwide scale, for the United Nations and all who seek to influence the rulers of the nations?

This train of thought brings us exactly to the point the Jews had reached in the first century. They had suffered under persecution and unjust rulers for many generations. Pagan monarchs had often tried to squeeze the life out of Judaism. Again and again they had pleaded with God that he would overthrow the oppressive tyrants and give them freedom, as he had done with Pharaoh at the time of the **Exodus**. But they had also learnt an important lesson about how to conduct themselves while waiting for God's deliverance. When they were in **exile** in Babylon, and longing for Babylon to be overthrown so they could go home again, the prophet Jeremiah (29.7) told them that during this waiting period they should settle down, live a normal life and *pray to God on behalf of Babylon*. If Babylon was at peace, they would be at peace.

I can just hear some zealous Christians objecting. It's a compromise! Surely we ought to be praying *against* pagan rulers. They exploit their subjects, they oppress people, they are wicked and should be overthrown. Well, in a sense, yes. But God's ways are not our ways, and his timing is not necessarily the timing we would like. Prophets may be called to preach against oppressive regimes. But for ordinary people it is better to be able to go about one's business, to live at peace, to raise a family, to be allowed to worship, without the awful insecurity that comes when governments are unstable or when different regimes follow one another in quick succession.

This was what many Jews of Jesus' day had realized. The Romans made all their subject peoples pray *to* the emperor, invoking him as lord and saviour. But they realized that this wouldn't work with the Jews, who believed that there was only one God; so they allowed them to pray *to* their own God *on behalf of* the emperor. This is the background to the early Christian attitude to praying for those in authority.

And notice how Paul puts it. Pray *for* all those in authority – because this is acceptable to 'God our saviour'! There is only one saviour, and it isn't Caesar, or any other human being, no matter how powerful they are. However surprising it may seem to us, praying for those in authority, even if they are pagan rulers, will become part of God's plan to spread the **gospel** to all the world. When rulers are doing their job, even if they don't acknowledge God themselves, they create the peace and social stability which will allow God's people to worship without being harassed, and to build up families and communities that follow the way of holiness.

In particular, when the world is at peace, the gospel can spread more easily. God wants people of every race, colour and language to come to him and find the true 'salvation'. Verses 4 and 7 indicate that praying for the peace of the world will be part of the apostolic mission to make this wider salvation a reality.

In the middle of it all, Paul restates his Jewish-style monotheism, to remind his hearers of the basis for this whole approach to prayer for rulers. The rulers are not divine, because there is only one God. Nor can any rulers claim that they are the human embodiment of a divine being, because there is only one person who stands as a 'mediator between God and humans', namely Jesus himself. Verse 5 is rather like 1 Corinthians 8.6: it offers an astonishing redefinition of Jewish monotheism, with Jesus in the middle of it. Like Jewish monotheism, this view of God is what prevents you worshipping earthly rulers, and encourages you instead to pray to God on their behalf. Unlike Jewish monotheism, the fact that this view of God is centred upon Jesus, who died as a ransom for the sins of the whole world (verse 6), means that the news of this one God, this one saviour, must now go out into all the world.

As so often in the New Testament, the call to prayer is also the call to think: to think clearly about God and the world, and God's project for the whole human race. Don't rest content with the simplistic agendas of the world that suggest you should either idolize your present political system or be working to overthrow it. Try praying for your rulers instead, and watch not only what God will do in your society but also how your own attitudes will grow, change and mature.

1 TIMOTHY 2.8–15

Women Must Be Allowed to Be Learners

> [8]So this is what I want: the men should pray in every place, lifting up holy hands, with no anger or disputing. [9]In the same way the women, too, should clothe themselves decently, being modest and sensible about it. They should not go in for elaborate hairstyles, or gold, or pearls, or expensive clothes. [10]Instead, as is appropriate for women who profess to be godly, they should adorn themselves with good works. [11]They must study undisturbed, in full submission to God. [12]I'm not saying that women should teach men, or try to dictate to them; rather, that they should be left undisturbed. [13]Adam was created first, you see, and then Eve; [14]and Adam was not deceived, but the woman was deceived, and fell into trespass. [15]She will, however, be kept safe through the process of childbirth, if she continues in faith, love and holiness with prudence.

As I write this, a short war has just finished in the Middle East. The newspapers have been full of it, and now they are picking over the details: was it really justified, who was to blame, did the invading armies fight according to the proper rules, and so on. But for the people who live in the country now devastated by the conflict there are more pressing concerns. Food, water and shelter are immediate problems; restoring law, order and social stability are major priorities. But while people are addressing these issues there are dangers lurking all around. Children pick up bright, shiny objects they find in the street . . . and some are blown to bits, while others, though they live to tell the tale, lose limbs or eyes or sustain permanent injury. Mines and unexploded bombs are a major hazard in many parts of the world, especially where there has been a war, even a short one. When people don't know what they are, they can be devastating. Even when the experts are called in, it's still quite dangerous.

There has been a different kind of war going on, in Western culture at least, for the last generation. It's been dubbed 'the war of the sexes', though it's not so much a battle between men and women as between different visions of what the roles of the two sexes should be in society, in marriage and in the church. Life becomes confusing at this point: some men are very much in favour of 'women's liberation', while some women are opposed to it. Passions run high. Those who grow up while it's all going on will discover soon enough that there are various parts of the traditional culture which are like unexploded bombs. Pick them up and they may go off in your hand.

In particular, there are several passages in the Bible which deal with the roles of men and women, and many people in modern Western culture don't like them. They accuse the biblical writers of being 'patri-archal', that is, of assuming that men should always run everything and that women should do what they're told, and of reinforcing this view in their writings. And this passage, particularly verse 12, is often held up as a prime example. Women mustn't be teachers, the verse seems to say; they mustn't hold any authority over men; they must keep silent. That, at least, is how many translations put it; indeed, this is the main passage people quote when they argue that the New Testament forbids the ordination of women. I was once reading these verses in a church service and a woman near the front exploded in anger, to the conster-nation of the rest of the congregation (even though some agreed with her). The whole passage seems to be saying that women are second-class citizens. They aren't even allowed to dress prettily. They are the daughters of Eve, and she was the original troublemaker. The best thing for them to do is to get on and have children, to behave them-selves and keep quiet.

That's how most people in our culture have read the passage. I acknowledge that the very different reading I'm going to suggest may sound, to begin with, as though I'm trying to make things easier, to tailor this bit of Paul to fit our culture. But there is good, solid scholar-ship behind what I'm going to say, and I genuinely believe it may be the right interpretation.

When you look at strip cartoons, B-grade movies and Z-grade nov-els and poems, you pick up a standard view of how 'everyone imag-ines' men and women behave. Men are macho, loud-mouthed, arrogant thugs, always fighting and wanting their own way. Women are sim-pering, empty-headed creatures, with nothing to think about except clothes and hairstyles and jewellery. There are 'Christian' versions of this, too: the men must make the decisions, run the show, always be in the lead, telling everyone what to do; women must stay at home, bring up the children and get the food ready. If you start looking for a biblical backup for this view, well, what about Genesis 3? Adam would never have sinned if Eve hadn't yielded first. Eve has her punishment, and it's pain in childbearing (Genesis 3.16).

Well, you don't have to embrace every aspect of the women's libera-tion movement to find that interpretation hard to swallow. Not only does it stick in our throat as a way of treating half the human race;

it doesn't fit with what we see in the rest of the New Testament, where women were the first witnesses of the **resurrection** (in other words, the first **apostles**); where Paul speaks of women as apostles and deacons (Romans 16); where he expects them to be praying and prophesying in the assembly (1 Corinthians 11), where 'there is no longer Jew or Greek; there is no longer slave or free; there is no "male and female"; you are all one in the Messiah, Jesus.' (Galatians 3.28). In particular, it doesn't fit with the practice of Jesus himself. In one telling little story (Luke 10.38–42) Mary of Bethany is sitting at Jesus' feet; in other words, she is joining the men in becoming a **disciple**, a learner, with a view to becoming a teacher in her turn. That's the main reason Martha was cross with her; no doubt she'd have liked some more help in the kitchen as well, but Mary's real offence was to cross a hidden barrier that, up to then, had kept women in the background and left education and leadership to the men.

The key to the present passage, then, is to recognize that it is commanding that women, too, should be allowed to study and learn, and should not be restrained from doing so (verse 11). They are to be 'in full submission'; this is often taken to mean 'to the men', or 'to their husbands', but it is equally likely that it refers to their attitude, as learners, of submission to God – which of course would be true for men as well. Then the crucial verse 12 need not be read as 'I do not allow a woman to teach or hold authority over a man' (the translation which has caused so much difficulty in recent years). It can equally mean: 'I don't mean to imply that I'm now setting up women as the new authority over men in the same way that previously men held authority over women.' Why might Paul need to say this?

There are some signs in the letter that it was originally sent to Timothy while he was in Ephesus. And one of the main things we know about religion in Ephesus is that the main religion – the biggest temple, the most famous shrine – was a female-only cult. The Temple of Artemis (that's her Greek name; the Romans called her Diana) was a massive structure which dominated the area. As befitted worshippers of a female deity, the **priests** were all women. They ruled the show and kept the men in their place.

Now if you were writing a letter to someone in a small, new religious movement with a base in Ephesus, and wanted to say that because of the **gospel** of Jesus the old ways of organizing male and female roles had to be rethought from top to bottom, with one feature of that being that the women were to be encouraged to study and learn and take a leadership role, you might well want to avoid giving the wrong impression. Was the apostle saying that women should be trained up so that Christianity would gradually become a cult like that of Artemis, where women did the leading and kept the men in line? That, it seems to me,

18

is what verse 12 is denying. The word I've translated 'try to dictate to them' is unusual, but seems to have the overtones of 'being bossy' or 'seizing control'. Paul is saying, like Jesus in Luke 10, that women must have the space and leisure to study and learn in their own way, not in order that they may muscle in and take over the leadership as in the Artemis cult, but so that men and women alike can develop whatever gifts of learning, teaching and leadership God is giving them.

What's the point of the other bits of the passage, then?

The first verse (8) is clear. The men must give themselves to devout prayer, and must not follow the normal stereotypes of 'male' behaviour: no anger or arguing. Then verses 9 and 10 follow, making the same point about the women. They must be set free from their stereotype, that of fussing all the time about hairdos, jewellery and fancy clothes – but they must be set free, not in order that they can be dowdy, unobtrusive little nobodies, but so that they can make a creative contribution to the wider society. The phrase 'good works' in verse 10 sounds bland to us, but it's one of the regular ways people used to refer to the social obligation to spend time and money on people less fortunate than oneself, to be a benefactor of the community through helping public works, the arts and so on.

Why then does Paul finish off with the explanation about Adam and Eve? Remember that his basic point is to insist that women, too, must be allowed to learn and study as Christians, and not be kept in unlettered, uneducated boredom and drudgery. Well, the story of Adam and Eve makes the point: look what happened when Eve was deceived. Women need to learn just as much as men do. Adam, after all, sinned quite deliberately; he knew what he was doing, he knew that it was wrong, and he deliberately went ahead. The Old Testament is very stern about that kind of action.

What about the bit about childbirth? Paul doesn't see it as a punishment. Rather, he offers an assurance that, though childbirth is indeed difficult, painful and dangerous, often the most testing moment in a woman's life, this is not a curse which must be taken as a sign of God's displeasure. God's salvation is promised to all, women and men alike, who follow Jesus in **faith**, love, holiness and prudence. And that includes those who contribute to God's creation through childbearing. Becoming a mother is hard enough, God knows, without pretending it's somehow an evil thing.

Let's not leave any more unexploded bombs and mines around for people to blow their minds with. Let's read this text as I believe it was intended, as a way of building up God's church, men and women, women and men alike. Just as Paul was concerned to apply this in one particular situation, so we must think and pray carefully about where our own cultures, prejudices and angers are taking us. We must do our best to conform, not to any of the different stereotypes the world offers, but to the healing, liberating, humanizing message of the gospel of Jesus.

1 TIMOTHY 3.1–7

The Character of a Bishop

> ¹Here is a trustworthy saying: if someone is eager for the work of overseeing God's people, the task they seek is a fine one. ²The bishop must be beyond reproach. He must not have more than one wife. He must be temperate, sensible, respectable, hospitable, a good teacher. ³He must not be a heavy drinker, or violent, but must be gentle, not quarrelsome, and not in love with money. ⁴He must be good at managing his own household, with his children being subject to him with all godliness. (⁵After all, if a man doesn't know how to run his own household, how can he take care of God's church?) ⁶He must not be a recent convert, in case he gets puffed up and falls into the devil's condemnation. ⁷In addition, he must have a good reputation with outsiders, so that he may not incur reproach and fall into the devil's snare.

A friend gave me a lift in the car the other night. He's a politician and has been a member of parliament for 25 years. But now he's decided to run for a new kind of public office: he's hoping to be a candidate to be Mayor of London.

'Suddenly,' he said to me, 'the party managers started asking me all kinds of questions about my private life. They never asked me questions like that when I wanted to be an MP. But if you're going to stand for a major position in the public eye they need to know that there's nothing which could bring the party into disrepute.' Not that his party is conservative in its attitude to personal morality; rather the opposite (though he himself is a lifelong practising Christian). But they know, as everyone in public life knows, that the higher you go up in an organization the more the world outside looks at you – at your personal character, your lifestyle, your family life – and will judge the organization itself by what they see of you.

That's why these instructions matter. If someone is to hold office within the church, their life must reflect what the church is all about. It's no good saying, 'But the church believes in forgiveness, therefore it doesn't matter if its leaders don't live up to the right standards, because that gives us a chance to show what we mean by forgiveness and new starts.' There are many today who use that line, but it doesn't work.

Christianity *is* indeed all about forgiveness, but the point of forgiveness is not that we can then relax and go on sinning because it'll all be all right somehow, but that God's forgiving love is meant to transform us into the new type of human beings which is what he longs to see. It's therefore vital that those who hold leadership positions should model the **gospel** message that there is a different way to be human, a different kind of lifestyle from what we see in the world all around.

Interestingly, it's a way of life which Paul expects outsiders to acknowledge as worthy. Many non-Christians will recognize when someone is living with the integrity proper to a **faith** in the living God, and will respect them for it – and will notice, likewise, when this isn't the case. Watch how the newspapers sneer at anyone in a position of public trust who fails to live up to that trust in their personal life. Trustworthiness is indivisible. The leader must therefore be 'beyond reproach'.

So who is Paul talking about here? I've translated the relevant word in two different ways in the first two verses. It literally means 'overseer', one who has a bird's-eye view of the church and is able to look after it as a whole. But from very early on – certainly by the end of the first century – the word had come to denote a particular office of leadership, the leadership given to one person in each community. (The question of how wide a geographical area that might cover is a separate issue which we can't comment on from this passage or letter.) And the word we normally use for this single leader in a community is 'bishop'.

This doesn't mean that the early church would have thought of 'bishops' in the way we do today. I happen to belong to a church that calls its senior leaders 'bishops', and many churches use that word, or its equivalent in other languages, to refer to the single person who has pastoral and teaching responsibility for an area including many different local churches. But it may be that to begin with the 'bishop' was simply the main leader, or perhaps even a member of a leadership team, in a local church – the pattern which is adopted in many 'non-episcopal' churches to this day. We can't be sure. However, the idea of a single person leading the church in an area which includes many local churches is certainly well established by early in the second century. It's quite possible that our present passage refers to this kind of office, perhaps as well as the main leader, or leaders, in a single community.

A further note on who this person is: Paul refers to the bishop throughout as a man. My reading of the rest of the New Testament inclines me to think that this is more because that's how Greek grammar normally refers to both genders together, and because in the very early days of the church the leaders of most communities were probably men. I don't see it as debarring women from this particular ministry and vocation.

So to the main point, and the main challenge, of this passage: what must this person be *like*? What are the special standards which they must uphold? In the light of what we said earlier, we should note that this isn't only of interest to those who are called to be office-holders (or those who want to check up on them); the reason they must keep to these standards is because this is what God longs to see all his children being like. The leaders must, as it were, be on the leading edge of that new humanity which the church is supposed to be. Because we're all 'on the way', rather than having 'made it' into the complete new humanity God desires, it's important that there are role models, especially that leaders should play that sort of part.

When it comes to specifics, Paul begins with the bishop's marital status: he must only have one wife. I don't think this means that the bishop should not have been married more than once (and have lost his wife through death or divorce and then married again). Polygamy was common in Paul's world, as it is in some parts of the world to this day. (The Old Testament, after all, has plenty of families like that, including some of the central figures in the story of God and Israel.) But Paul has grasped, following the words of Jesus in Mark 10 and elsewhere, that God's long-term plan, intended from the very beginning, was for faithful, lifelong partnerships of one man and one woman. That is what church leaders should model.

Nor do I think this means that the bishop *must* be married, in other words, that single people are ruled out. Different churches have different norms at this point. What is being ruled out is a person in a position of leadership who has two or more wives. This is all the more interesting because it implies that there were some, perhaps many, people in the early Christian churches who did have two or more wives – just as there are some converts in churches in Africa, for example, who have come from a background where polygamy is normal. Debates rage today about whether such people should be told to choose one wife only and dismiss the others, or whether, as the present passage seems to me to imply, they should be accepted as members of the church as they are, but should not be put in a position of leadership where they would then be regarded as role models.

I realize this is tricky because it seems to set up two different standards – a special level of holiness for the 'clergy', and a lower one for everybody else. That can be disastrous. Any 'ordinary Christian' who thinks they can leave the practice of real holiness to the 'professionals' is heading for disaster. But I return to the point I made at the beginning. Of course God wants all his people to embody the life of the new creation which has begun in Jesus and is available through the power of the **spirit**. He longs that every single one of us should follow after that holiness as energetically as we can. But as every pastor and teacher knows, different people make progress at different rates. In any real community, as opposed to theoretical ones that people hold in their heads while reading texts, there are anomalies and puzzles, times when you have to accept that at the moment a particular situation is not ideal, but it's where we are. The point, though, shines out all the more clearly: those in leadership positions should not exhibit that kind of anomaly. Their lives must embody and represent the **message** they are called upon to proclaim.

The rest of the instructions follow the same pattern. We might want to highlight, as the previous passage did, the ways in which normal cultural expectations of male behaviour are challenged by the command of the gospel. 'Gentleness' wasn't regarded as much of a male virtue in the ancient world, and it still isn't in many places. That's important when it comes to managing one's own household, and also to managing God's church. It's not too difficult to manage a community by bullying and bossing everyone around, and losing your temper and threatening violence when people step out of line. But if you do that you will not only cause human disasters; you will hold up a rotten picture to the world and the church of what the gospel of Jesus is like.

The last two notes are particularly important. Pride is such an easy trap to fall into that the church must take care not to expose people to its dangers too soon. And, once again, the leader must be well thought of in the community beyond the church. Obviously at a time of persecution the entire church may be vilified by outsiders. But in relatively calm periods people around will watch this strange little group who don't behave the way everyone else does. They want to know if they are good neighbours, good citizens, good friends. That isn't the whole Christian duty towards outsiders, of course. The responsibility to preach the gospel remains central. But people are much more likely to listen to what we say if they like what they see of who we are. And if that's true for ordinary church members, how much more for leaders. Especially bishops.

1 TIMOTHY 3.8–13

The Character of Deacons

⁸In the same way, deacons must be serious-minded, not the sort of people who say one thing today and another tomorrow, not heavy drinkers, not eager for shameful gain. ⁹They must hold on to the

mystery of the faith with a pure conscience. [10]They must first be
tested; then, when they have been found without reproach, they may
serve as deacons. [11]The womenfolk, too, should be serious-minded,
not slanderers, but temperate and faithful in all things. [12]Deacons
should have only one wife, and should be well in charge of their children and their own households. [13]Those who serve well as deacons,
you see, gain a good platform for themselves to speak out boldly in
the faith which is in Messiah Jesus.

We had just begun to taxi out to the runway, and I was settling back in
my seat and wondering what the airline might come up with for lunch.
Suddenly the plane stopped. After a short pause, the captain came on
the intercom. 'Sorry, folks', he said, sounding as irritated as we were all
about to be. 'Just got word. There's a small electrical fault. It's nothing
serious but we have to fix it. We've got to go back to the gate and call
the technician. Should be about twenty minutes.'

Well, the twenty minutes turned into thirty, then into an hour, and
eventually the frustrated passengers were invited to leave the plane,
go back into the terminal, and have a free drink at the cafe. Better
than nothing but not what we wanted. I remember being struck by the
absolute rule about turning back for even a minor fault. It wouldn't
have affected the flight. It wouldn't have made the plane unsafe. But I
would much rather err on the side of appropriate caution, even when it
means the anticlimax of going back to the same airport lounge you left
two hours earlier. And it set me thinking about some of the things in
church life about which the New Testament tells us we should regularly
be running checks.

Like the character of church leaders, for instance. This passage turns
from 'bishops' – who seem here to be the senior leaders or pastors –
to 'deacons', a word which basically means 'servants'. Of course, all
Christians are called to serve one another, and this applies especially to
those in leadership positions. But from very early on (the story is told
in Acts 6), the church appointed some people to organize and administer the practical details of daily living within the renewed people of
God. This didn't mean that they were not themselves also to be teachers; in fact one of the very first 'deacons', Stephen, seems quickly to have
become one of the most powerful speakers in the early church, attract-
ing such negative attention that he became the first person to be killed
for his outspoken Christian stand. The present passage seems to envisage deacons having the same opportunity to speak up for the **gospel**.
Their administrative duties are important; but ideally, as verse 13 says,
that work should have the effect of bringing them into the sort of prom-
inence and respect that will gain a hearing for what they will then say.

The main point of the passage is the series of tests the church should run on a person's character before he or she is allowed to hold office (verse 10), like the airline pilot running tests on all the systems prior to take-off. As we saw in the previous passage, those who hold office in any organization, whether it's a bank or a golf club or a restaurant or a church, are expected to model the kind of behaviour appropriate for all the members. If they don't – if, for instance, the secretary of the golf club makes a habit of driving his car across the green in front of the clubhouse – ordinary members will quickly get the message that nobody cares how you behave. And the kind of checks to be run on church leaders, according to this passage, have to do with the sorts of thing which, once the plane gets airborne – once the person is in office, in other words – it's a bit late to be worrying about. Dismissing an office-holder is difficult, and sends nasty shock waves through the whole community. Much better to find out in advance if there are residual weaknesses which need to be addressed.

The first of these tests concerns the person's state of mind and how it appears in their speech. Some people always seem to be flitting from one topic to another, and then, forgetting what they just said, say the opposite the next day. Some are flippant, always turning serious subjects into a joke as though to imply that nothing really matters that much. 'Serious-minded', in verses 8 and 11 (the fact that it's repeated shows how important it is), doesn't mean 'gloomy'. Rather, it means the practised habit of concentrating properly on things that matter instead of going through life ignoring the important issues. Paul uses a single word where I've translated 'say one thing today and another tomorrow'; his word means, literally, 'double-worded'. I was with someone the other day who reported to me a conversation he'd had with a third person, but when, later on, the third person also spoke to me, I got a totally different picture of what had been said. That kind of behaviour totally undermines trust and community health. Those who take office in the church, including the most basic administrative tasks, must be people whose characters have been formed in truth-telling and consistent speech.

Drink and money come next. Paul doesn't say that office-bearers shouldn't drink alcohol, but he is quite clear that they should know when to stop – which, as experience shows, frequently means 'one drink before you think you should'. In Paul's world, as in some parts of our own, clean and healthy drinking water would be hard to come by, and wine would be the natural, cheap and appropriate option for many people much of the time. The point comes up again in verse 23 of chapter 5. But as with many good things, there are dangers lurking round the corner, in this case that of self-indulgence. There is an essential immaturity about heavy drinking: someone who treats their own body in that way is hardly likely to be the sort of person you'd trust to treat other people and their property in a responsible fashion.

And as for money – well, anyone who has been involved with any organization for very long, including sadly the church, is bound to notice the close, and awkward, connection of money and power. Those who handle money find that it brings power, a power with which they must be extremely careful. (The church treasurer is often in a position to comment on whether the church can really afford to do this or that, and is often tempted to find ways of affording the projects he or she supports while declaring that others will break the bank.) Equally, those who hold power, even in the small world of a church fellowship, often find that it provides them with an opportunity to make money. Let's not draw the wrong conclusions from this; later on in the letter (5.17) Paul will insist on proper payment for good work. But those appointed to office must be the sort of people who are already known as restrained, responsible and reliable. They must not be the sort of people who will be watching out for extra chances of using their position to line their own pockets.

All this leads to the larger statement in verse 9, repeating 1.5: deacons must hold on to the mystery of the **faith** with a pure conscience. This is like saying that a vase (a) must not leak and (b) must be placed on a firm base in case it falls over. Church leaders must have a firm grasp on the central mystery of the faith; as they do so, there must be no hidden moral problems which will cause them to topple over as they bear public witness. Saying that they must keep their consciences pure doesn't mean they will never sin, or make mistakes; only that they must keep short and honest accounts with God, and (where appropriate) with the church.

Verse 11 raises a difficult question. Some people think it refers to the womenfolk within a deacon's household, in other words specifically the wife of a deacon – assuming 'deacons' in this early period were always male. Others, pointing out the parallel between verses 8 and 11, think that the women in question are women deacons, such as we find (for instance) in the case of Phoebe in Romans 16.1. The question remains at least open. One way or another, it's clear that the women were not regarded as silent onlookers, but as people with roles to play and responsibilities to be, in their own right, people of exemplary Christian character.

As with the bishops in verses 1–7, the deacons must be people whose families, too, are in good order. It shouldn't need saying that this doesn't mean a repressed, fearful family discipline which squashes everyone into the same narrow mould. Families must be places of life and joy and fun as well as mutual support in good times and bad. But they must also be places where appropriate discipline and respect for one another are modelled. If deacons can't achieve that within their own households, it's not likely that they will make it happen within the church.

The tests are stringent but necessary. I'd rather wait for the next plane than set off in one which had a single loose screw.

1 TIMOTHY 3.14–16

The Mystery of Godliness

[14]I'm writing this to you in the hope that I'll be able to come to you in the near future. [15]But, if I'm delayed, this will help you to know how people should behave in God's household, which is the assembly of the living God, the pillar and firm foundation of the truth. [16]Indeed, the mystery of godliness is certainly great:

> He was revealed in the flesh,
> and vindicated in the spirit;
> he appeared to angels,
> and was announced to Gentiles;
> he was believed in the world,
> and taken up in glory.

The senior officer investigating the case consulted his colleagues once more, and then went out to speak to the waiting press. 'I'm sorry to say', he said, 'that the incident remains a complete mystery. There is no explanation for what happened. We have no leads to go on. Unless something new comes to light, a mystery it is and a mystery it will remain.'

Watching this on television, I found it deeply frustrating, not just because the murder in question affected many people who were now going to be left without answers to their questions, but because the thought of something so totally inexplicable poses an affront to any historian. But I also found it interesting because of the way the word 'mystery' has come to be used today. We think of it as meaning, in the policeman's words, something for which there is 'no explanation': something we can't understand and probably never will.

That is, indeed, not far from the meaning the word had for people in Paul's day (the Greek word he uses is effectively the same, *mysterion*). But there was an all-important twist to it. In many of the popular religions in Paul's world (and if 1 Timothy was written while Timothy was in Ephesus this would be especially relevant, since Ephesus was a bubbling melting pot of popular religions) the idea of a 'mystery' was not just something you couldn't understand; it was something that *most* people couldn't and didn't understand, but that some did – though they, of course, kept it secret so that everyone else would stay in the dark.

'Mysteries' of this sort were only revealed to the inner circle, to those who had been initiated into the religion. They were a kind of secret code, the secret to the meaning of life, the universe, God, everything; the secret, too, to someone's own life, the hidden clue that would make sense of everything and bring you peace of mind, salvation, or whatever else the religion in question might be offering. And some of these 'mysteries' came in secret formulae, magical verses which you might be taught and which you would repeat as a kind of prayer or mantra, reminding yourself of the hidden truths and hoping that they would transform your life.

The Christian 'religion', as it made its way within this world of many religions, must have seemed to many people one religion among many. That wasn't how Paul and the other **apostles** would have seen it, because for them it was first and foremost the fulfilment of the sharp-edged promises made by the One True God to Israel – and the God of Israel towered above the pagan 'gods' in the way Mount Everest towers over a tiny Himalayan village. But all the same Paul and the other early teachers were ready to take people on in the terms they were used to; and that's what we find in verse 16. So, they say, it's 'mysteries' you want, is it? You're eager for hidden knowledge, the secrets of the universe, the formula that'll change your life? Well, here's the 'mystery' that's now revealed to all the world! You can have it in a formula, a brief, six-line poetic jingle, which might even sound a bit like the kind of 'mystery' you had known elsewhere . . . but this isn't just one 'mystery' among others. This is the real thing. This isn't just a secret, it's a story; not just any old story, but the true story, the story of the God who became human and who now rules the whole world as its rightful Lord. This 'mystery' won't lead you into a secret, private 'religion'. It will change your life all right – by leading you out into a new way of life, a way of service and **faith** and discipleship and hope.

The 'mystery' is, of course, the story of Jesus **Christ**, though he isn't mentioned by name in the six-line jingle. The lines aren't meant to be in order; this little verse isn't like Philippians 2.6–11, which tells the story of Jesus from the time before his birth through to his glorification. It looks as though each pair of lines has been chosen to balance its neighbour: flesh/**spirit**, angels/**Gentiles**, world/glory. Each pair invites the reader – or perhaps we should say the prayer, since a little formula like this was certainly meant to be prayed, not just thought about – to mull it over in the presence of God, to allow the strange contrasts to demolish the normal assumptions about how the world worked, how human **life** worked, how (so to speak) God worked, and to build up a new picture with Jesus at the middle of it. Let's look briefly at each pair.

'Revealed in the flesh and justified in the spirit'! The idea of any divine being making an appearance in human *form* would have been exciting enough for most people in the ancient world; but the Christians went further. The one they worshipped had actually *become* flesh, become genuinely human, capable of laughter and tears, of suffering and dying. But after this death God had vindicated him, by the creator spirit through whose power Jesus was raised from the dead; that's what 'justified in the spirit' means. Thus the mystery opens with the central statements of Christian faith, putting the basic **gospel** message into somewhat cryptic language: Christ died for our sins, and was raised.

'Appeared to angels, announced to Gentiles.' Jesus has gone ahead of his people into God's sphere, into **heaven**, until the time when he is revealed once more. There he is to this day, in the place where the angels live. But this doesn't mean he's absent, just a distant memory. No: he is 'announced' to the Gentiles, the pagan nations, the non-Jewish peoples. And the word 'announced' is the word you might use, not so much of a new religion you were trying to spread, but of a new emperor you were summoning them to obey, and perhaps even to worship. As we see at various stages of the Pastoral Letters, Paul gently nudges his readers towards recognizing that the 'religious' figure whom Jesus supersedes above all is the most powerful one of the day: not Zeus or Aphrodite, not Diana or Apollo, but Caesar himself, 'announced' to the whole world as its true lord, summoning the world to obey and (in some parts of the empire at least) to worship him.

'Believed in the world, taken up in glory'. Once more we have the earthly and the heavenly stories sitting side by side. The word 'believe' is a rich one for Paul and the early Christians; it involves trust and loyalty as well as what we call 'religious' faith or belief in particular doctrines. Whoever wrote this little 'mystery' was celebrating the fact that Jesus wasn't just being announced to the wider world; people were giving him their believing allegiance. And rightly so. He was the one who, having been exalted to glory, was now already ruling the world as its genuine Lord.

What has happened in this formula, as we can now see, is that a great deal of Christian faith and truth has been compressed into a small number of words (there are 18 in Greek). They deserve careful pondering in prayer and reflection. They capture, in however teasing a fashion, the rich flavour of early Christian spirituality – and the way in which it challenged both the popular 'mysteries' and the ever-expanding rule of Caesar.

The point of it all in the present passage is that people who base their lives on this strange but powerful 'mystery', people who allow their own personal story to be reshaped around the story of Jesus himself, discover that they are 'the assembly of the living God', as opposed to the various gatherings of the 'gods' of popular culture. As they discover that, they may be startled to learn that they are themselves, as a community, to be the stabilizing force that helps God's truth to stand up and be seen in the world. If the church is founded solidly on God's truth, what people see and know of God's truth will be based on the life and witness of God's people. That's why this letter is being written, as verses 14 and 15 make clear: so that, in the apostle's absence, the church may nevertheless learn what it means to share a common life, grounded in the mystery of Christ, through which the watching world can see who its rightful Lord really is.

1 TIMOTHY 4.1–5

Beware of False Teaching!

> ¹Now the spirit specifically declares that in the last times some people will abandon the faith, and will cling on to deceitful spirits and demonic teachings ²perpetrated by hypocritical false teachers whose consciences are branded with a hot iron. ³They will forbid marriage, and teach people to abstain from foods which God created to be received with thanksgiving by people who believe and know the truth. ⁴Every creation of God, you see, is good; nothing is to be rejected if it is received with thanksgiving, ⁵for then it is made holy by God's word and prayer.

Jane grew up in a family which was always playing games. Outdoor games, whenever possible; but if the weather was bad, and especially on long winter evenings, the children would curl up around the fire and play – well, you name it: Scrabble, Monopoly, Cluedo of course, and lots of other board games. But best of all they liked the old-fashioned card games. They liked the feel of the cards; the excitement of having them dealt out and looking eagerly to see whether they'd got a good hand or not. They got to know the different faces of the Jack, Queen and King of each suit, and the most special cards of all, the Aces. They even had nicknames for them. In later years they would look back and realize that what they might have missed out on, in those days before television, they had more than made up for in terms of exercising their memories, their ability to think strategically, and, equally important, their readiness to play the hand they'd been dealt and not grumble because someone else had a better one.

It was only when Jane met James and got to know his family that she realized for the first time that not everybody saw playing cards in that way. James's grandfather had lost his job in the Depression, and the family had had to move into a small house in a shabby neighbourhood. In desperation, casting about wildly for some way to recover financial stability and provide for his family, he had gone one evening into a bar where people were gambling for money. But what began as a last desperate measure quickly became an obsession. The Jack, Queen and King imprisoned him in their castle, and he broke the hearts of his family instead of bringing them back the diamonds he had hoped. James's father had grown up in a household where the very sight of playing cards reminded them of folly, shame, ridicule and ruin.

Now of course people can, and do, gamble on anything. And some people, it seems, can have (as they say) a mild 'flutter' on horses, dogs, cards or whatever without it becoming a habit, let alone a destructive one. But social fashions have associated some things so closely with gambling, and gambling so closely with irresponsible, immoral and ruinous behaviour, that the very objects themselves – pasteboard cards with lifeless decorations – have been seen by some as 'tainted' and so to be avoided.

This helps us to understand the position Paul is describing in verses 2 and 3, and the teaching he offers against it in verses 4 and 5. In the early church, and in many later parts of Christianity, there were some whose experience of the pagan world had been very destructive. In particular, they had been used to engaging in wild and profligate sex, drunken orgies of various kinds. Modern as well as ancient experience suggests that when people go in for that kind of behaviour in a serious way it turns out to be destructive, and they know in their bones that this is not how humans were made to live. Something in you dies when you give yourself indiscriminately to gluttony, whether in food, drink or sex. And we can easily understand – not least because several people have written frankly about it in their own experience – that people who go that route may well end up hating the very thought of good food, of alcoholic drinks or indeed of sex. People like that, Paul says, have had their consciences branded as though with a hot iron. The inner guiding light that ought to be telling them that some things are good and other things are bad has been so mistreated that it now winces with pain at the very thought of some things which are perfectly all right in themselves, part of the good creation of a good creator God.

This, in fact, is the underlying point, and it needs making again and again in almost every generation. If in doubt, read Genesis 1: God saw all that he made, *and it was very good*. That is the foundation of all genuine Christian (and for that matter Jewish) thinking. Anything which implies that some part of the created order is bad in itself is the first swish of the axe which will cut off the branch on which we should be sitting – the belief that the God who made the world in the first place is remaking it through Jesus and the **spirit**, and that we are called, not to abandon our humanity but to celebrate its rescue, redemption and remaking. What we see in this passage is one of the early signs of a problem which dogged the footsteps of Christian thinkers through much of the early period, and reappears from time to time today – though frankly the modern Western church is often in danger of going to the opposite extreme, so keen on emphasizing how good the world is that it fails to see that there is just as much danger in *abusing* the created order as there is in regarding it as evil. Thinking clearly at this point is basic to grown-up Christian living.

In particular, it's fascinating that already by the time of this letter Paul could see that some would end up saying that sex itself is simply bad, so that ideally all people should be celibate. Some have even charged Paul himself with taking this view, though a more careful reading of 1 Corinthians 7, the key passage, will show how wrong that is. And when it came to food and drink, Paul took the robust view that *nothing* was unclean in itself – including the foods that the Old Testament had prohibited, and including meat that had been offered in **sacrifice** to idols. That's the point of 1 Corinthians 8—10, though as that passage makes clear he is equally insistent that Christians must give up their rights to eat whatever they like if it weakens the **faith** of another Christian. But the underlying point is the one to grasp: creation is good; created pleasures, in their proper and appropriate form and context, are to be received with thanksgiving.

Thanksgiving – one of the major themes of Paul's letter to the Colossians – is more than just a recognition of the fact that we receive everything from the hands of a loving God. It is the fundamental human and Christian stance, poised between God and creation. It simultaneously renounces idolatry – treating the created order as if it were itself divine – and the dualism which treats creation as shabby or bad. When we thank God, we grow to our proper stature. That's why those who reject creation, just like those who idolize it, must be seen as deceitful and even demonic (verse 1). Finding our way down the straight path between worshipping creation and rejecting it may be difficult from time to time. But thanksgiving – coupling God's **word**, which affirms the goodness of creation, with grateful prayer – is the key to it all.

1 TIMOTHY 4.6–10

Get into Training!

⁶Set these instructions before the family. If you do this, you will be a good servant of Messiah Jesus; you will be nourished by the words of faith and the good teaching which you have been following. ⁷Keep well away from worthless myths, the sort of things some old women mumble on about.

Go into training in godliness! ⁸Physical exercise, you see, has a limited usefulness, but godliness is useful in every way. It carries the promise of life both now and in the future. ⁹That saying is trustworthy; it deserves to be accepted totally! ¹⁰This is what we are working and struggling for, you see, because we have set our hope on the living God, who is the saviour of all people – more especially, of believers.

The last time I made a serious effort to get physically fit I had a specific purpose in mind. We were about to launch into a complicated move of house, and I knew that I was going to be on my feet all day for a long time, carrying boxes, books, pictures and goodness knows what else. I was going to be climbing ladders and moving furniture, not to mention sorting out a garden. I needed to go into training, and I did. It worked. I really ought to be doing it again now . . .

Verse 8 is one of the clearest references to physical exercise in the New Testament. As in the previous passage, there are echoes of 1 Corinthians here, in this case of 9.24–27; there, Paul mentions athletics, wrestling, running races and boxing, all familiar sports in his world. Whether Timothy was actively involved in that kind of thing we can't tell, since verse 8 may just be a powerful illustration rather than a comment on what he's actually doing, but the point is obvious: for genuine godliness, true piety, you need to go into training just as much as an athlete does. And this sort of training is even more worthwhile. The first will make you physically fit, able (at least in principle) to work harder and enjoy life more. The second will make you . . . well, not just spiritually fit (as though the point of it all was to be able to engage in a more energetic spiritual life), but the kind of person who reflects God's image, one who has taken him – or herself in hand, has seen the need to develop properly as a fully human being, and taken appropriate action. This, as we shall see presently, is what Paul means by **life**.

This is emphatically not what people today expect or want to hear. We expect and want to be told that 'spirituality' is simply the sense I have of being in God's presence, being surrounded with his love, sensing a transcendent dimension in the affairs of everyday life. It comes as a shock to be told that it's something you have to *work* at – and something, moreover, which will take the same kind of hard work as going into training for athletics, or even in order to move house.

Paul doesn't say what kind of exercises he has in mind, though many wise guides have developed such things. But he does refer, in verse 10, to his own hard work and struggles, and the word 'struggle' is the regular one wrestlers would use. This is how Paul understands the work of prayer, pastoral care and evangelism: not as a smooth, easy set of tasks, the kind of thing that just flows naturally, but as something through which one is changed the way that a block of marble is changed, as the sculptor chips away at it to get to the beautiful statue she has in mind, and as something through which the world around is changed, in the way that a hard-working labourer can transform a plot of thistles and nettles into a lovely garden.

The garden he's working on – or, if you prefer, the sculpture he's chiselling out – has a grand name: life (verse 8). The power of death, decay and deconstruction is so strong that if life, the new life that God longs to give to his whole creation, is to win, it must involve and engage all the energies of God's people in working for it. This God is the living God (as opposed to the lifeless, powerless gods of popular mythology). Those who struggle and wrestle in their spiritual exercises under his direction are doing so in order to attain the ultimate life of the new world itself, and also the anticipation of that life which comes forward to meet us in the present.

As they do so, they need to be reminded more sharply of who this God is and what he's done. He is, says Paul, 'the saviour of all people, more especially of believers' (verse 10). This has given rise to three different interpretations.

Some think Paul is saying that everyone will be 'saved', in the full, final sense, but that those who believe the **gospel** in the present already enjoy salvation here and now and so have a fuller 'salvation' than those who don't.

Others, recognizing that Paul regularly warns that some will *not* be saved at the last, think that he's saying only that God is in principle, and potentially, the saviour for everyone. In other words, there is no other saviour; anyone who does want to be saved will have to be saved by him rather than by someone else; but in fact the only people who are saved are believers.

Others again – and I think this is the best option – note that the word 'saviour' was in regular use in Paul's world as a title of honour for Caesar, the Roman emperor. In using it for God, as here, or for Jesus, as in 2 Timothy 1.10, Paul is making a claim that this God, and this Jesus, are the true 'saviour' in the sense that through them the whole world will be rescued from decay and injustice. There is a sense in which the entire world, and all people in it, are better off as a result of the saving work of God through Jesus. But, since humans retain the right and dignity to refuse God's ultimate offer, it is only believers who appropriate this salvation fully.

The main command of this paragraph, though, comes at the beginning. A central part of pastoral work, of looking after the community of God's people, is *teaching*: instructing, feeding with the truth, laying things out in a clear and wholesome way so that people can understand what this strange new way of life really is to which they have been called in the gospel. We desperately need this today, as so many assume that Christianity is simply a way of being 'religious' from time to time, while the rest of life goes on in tune with the world around. Alternatively (and we see this today as well), many are looking for a religious teaching that appears exotic, exciting and esoteric. They are prepared to listen to anyone who has some strange new idea. Paul dismisses this with a wave of the hand. There are lots of odd myths out there, the kind of thing that people like to mumble on about, but you must avoid them. There is such a thing as healthy, nutritious teaching. Those who are getting into training in godliness will have a good appetite for it.

1 TIMOTHY 4.11–16

Pay Attention to Yourself and Your Teaching

> [11]You must urge and teach these things. [12]Don't let anyone look down on you because you are young, but be an example to the believers in what you say, how you behave, in love, faith and holiness. [13]Until I come, give attention to reading, to exhortation and to teaching. [14]Don't neglect the gift that is in you, which was given to you through prophecy when the elders laid hands on you. [15]Work hard at these things; give yourself to them, so that everyone may see your progress. [16]Pay attention to yourself and your teaching, and keep steadily on with them. If you do that, you see, you will save yourself, and those who hear you as well.

I listened as the great scientist brought his lecture to its climax. He had ranged across the universe, explored tiny life forms on the one hand and vast tracts of intergalactic space on the other. He had spoken of the theories that tried to bring it all together and of the wonders that were yet to be explored. 'And yet,' he said, 'wherever we look, whether it's in the most powerful microscope, studying subatomic particles, or whether it's through the most powerful telescope, exploring objects millions of light years away, the most fascinating thing in the whole universe remains that which is two inches this side of the lens.'

It was a salutary – and exciting – reminder of the challenging truth. We human beings, tiny compared with the universe, large and clumsy compared to the smallest life forms, contain within ourselves something which is more fascinating, dare we say more precious, than anything else yet discovered in our world. We have a kind of **life**, and a self-conscious life at that, of a depth and complexity that when we stop to ponder it we are sometimes overwhelmed by its mystery.

If we humans as a race need from time to time to stop looking outward and remind ourselves who we really are, the same is true, in a more specialized sense, of those who work for God and the **gospel**. It is quite possible to spend every waking hour – and some of the sleeping ones as well – worrying away at the numerous tasks which the pastor and preacher and church organizer has to attend to. There are sermons to write, hymns and music to choose and perhaps arrange, assistants to consult, decisions to be made. There are people in distress, people in joy, people in rebellion against the gospel, people facing disaster, people living with disease and trouble and fear and anger . . . and the pastor and preacher wants to be there for all of them, wants to help all of them, wants to carry them on her or his heart before God. Then – and this may well be the first thing on the mind – there are neighbours who object to cars being parked near the church; there are local councils who don't want the church bells to be rung; there are unemployed young people who throw stones through the church windows. And every day the newspapers and television bring news of another war, another international crisis, the problems of global debt, the unhealed sore of asylum-seekers and refugees, and a thousand other things to which the church, locally as well as globally, must give attention. As a pastor and preacher myself, just writing this paragraph has made me feel tired.

Those called to Christian ministry may well feel that their task is never to think of themselves. There's a world out there, there's a church out there, and we are simply its servants. That is of course true at one level, as many passages in the New Testament insist (look, for example, at 2 Corinthians 4.5). But at the same time one of the major problems in the church over the last few decades has been clergy burnout – a vivid and nasty metaphor for the horrible reality of combined physical exhaustion, emotional distress (feeling you've let everyone down), family disaster (overworked clergy sometimes ignore their family until it's too late), the possibility of losing your job, and, not least, the sense that you ought to be setting the church a good example but you're doing the opposite.

Faced with this dilemma, our present passage gives clear, strong and wise advice. 'Give attention to reading, to exhortation and to teaching.' 'Don't neglect the gift that is in you.' 'Pay attention to yourself and your teaching.' Each of these is important, and easily overlooked when you're under pressure. Verse 12 warns Timothy not to let anyone look down on him because he's young; he must keep his nerve, and trust that God will be at work through him when he does what he's been called to do, not when he tries to do nineteen things he hasn't been called to do. Some clergy feel the pressure of their youth, not least in the kind of parish where the average age of the congregation is at least twice their own. 'We've been here in this church for fifty years,' they seem to be saying, 'and don't you try to tell us what to think or do!' But there are other pressures, too, on clergy, not least because most of the time they are not directly responsible to anybody else; nobody is telling them to do these four things this morning, those five this afternoon, and to finish off the rest this evening. Rather, a generalized mass of possible tasks stares up at them from a crowded desk and a flashing answerphone. How many people, faced with all that, will have the courage to obey even the first of Paul's instructions?

'Give attention to reading!' For most of us, including people like me who have spent a lifetime in academic and church work, reading is the thing we only allow ourselves to do as a kind of luxury when the urgent things are done. It's all too easy to let books, journals and so on pile up and then try to read several of them on a train or a plane, or a day which ought really to be a proper day off. Yet here it is at the top of the list. How are we to obey?

Part of the problem is that in modern Western culture reading *feels* like a form of relaxation rather than a form of work. Even if the book is demanding, and you need to make notes as you go along, you may find it easiest to sit in an armchair, perhaps with a cup of coffee, maybe with music in the background. How, you feel, can you possibly justify spending hours of a working day in such a posture? Yet reading is a form of renunciation, almost a living embodiment of the call to **faith** over against works: you must renounce your strenuous efforts to justify your existence by the busy-busy lifestyle that pastors regularly fall into. I hope this present book will be read by people who are not pastors as well as those who are, and I hope such non-clergy readers will take it upon themselves to enquire sensitively about the pastor's reading habits, and to find ways of adjusting church structures and expectations so that reading becomes a priority. Congregations who do that can expect, for a start, more interesting sermons; but that's just the start. A pastor with a ready, receptive mind, open to lifelong learning, will be a gift that keeps on giving to those in her or his care.

A gift, indeed; and that's the point of the second instruction. God gives specific gifts to each of his children, and it's specially important that those called to ordained ministry should be aware of the gifts they have and take care to cultivate them. They are not for our own benefit, but for that of the whole wider church, which as verse 15 indicates should rejoice to see gifts developed, like plants taking root and flourishing in a well-stocked garden.

But in the middle of it all is the instruction clergy find it hardest to hear. Pay attention *to yourself*. What sort of a person are you becoming? Are you like someone giving classes on car maintenance while driving around in a dangerous, battered old banger? Are you like a music teacher too busy to tune your own violin? Are you like the leader of a mountain expedition who's forgotten to bring your own walking boots? Of course there is a danger of being obsessed with yourself ('me and my ministry'). Of course some people today spend too much time navel-gazing. For most of us that's not the problem. 'Give attention'. 'Be diligent'. 'Pay attention'. All those commands sound threatening. But once you see what they're saying, they are in fact liberating. Go ahead! Embrace and enjoy the true freedom of serving God and his people.

1 TIMOTHY 5.1–8

Human Families and God's Family

> [1]Don't rebuke a senior man in the church, but exhort him as you might do with your father – or, in the case of younger ones, with your brothers. [2]Treat the older women as mothers, and the younger ones as sisters, with all purity.
>
> [3]Pay respect to widows who really are widows. [4]If a widow has children or grandchildren, let them first learn to respect their own family and to make some repayment to those who brought them up. This, you see, pleases God. [5]A real widow is one who, left by herself, has set her hope on God, and continues in prayer and supplication night and day; [6]but a self-indulgent woman is dead even while she's alive. [7]Give these commands so that they may be beyond blame. [8]If anyone doesn't take care of their own relatives, especially their own household, they have denied the faith; they are worse than unbelievers.

I know a wonderful couple who have eleven children. Mind you, they didn't have eleven together. His first wife died; her first husband died; they then met and married; and when they put his six and her five together, lo and behold, they had enough for a football team.

Imagine how you'd feel as one of the eleven. There are all kinds of new dynamics. Suddenly your family has more or less doubled in size, and you have to get used to being part of a household, doing regular chores, discovering one another's likes and dislikes, learning how to respect and value each other and not impose on or exploit one another. Extended families provide endless possibilities for tensions and difficulties as well as for friendship, fun and mutual support.

The early church did its best to live as a kind of extended family. This comes as a surprise to those who don't look closely enough at Paul's letters. People often assume that the remarkable life of the Jerusalem church as described in Acts (e.g. 2.43–47) was a kind of early experiment that didn't really work and so wasn't repeated. Certainly we don't find Paul telling people that they should sell their property and pool their resources. But what we do find, in various places, is the command to care for one another. This doesn't just mean thinking kind thoughts and saying comforting words. It means providing material and financial help for those in need.

In particular, in a world without any form of state-organized social welfare, the church from the very beginning took upon itself the task of caring for those with nobody to look after them and no means of supporting themselves. This meant, in particular, widows. In the ancient world, women whose husbands had died often faced total destitution. Often, when someone became a Christian, their own family would disown them, so that any support from relatives would be cut off. The church faced the task of living as an alternative family, and had to come to terms with the resulting tensions and difficulties, as well as the possibilities of joyful shared life and mutual support.

This is why, in the present passage and the next one, Paul goes into considerable detail on the rules for enrolling and supporting widows. I remember that once, when I was a student, and first coming to grips with Paul's thought, a friend said to me that he couldn't believe that Paul wrote 1 Timothy 'because', he said, 'Paul was interested in justification by faith, in the death of Jesus, and things like that – and all that fussing about widows seems so trivial by comparison'. I didn't have a good answer for him at the time, but I can think of two now.

First, if you think that helping someone who's destitute is trivial compared with abstract doctrinal debates, however important they may be in their own place, something is wrong with the way you're looking at God and the world. Second, the reason Paul is concerned about widows is directly and intimately related to his whole view of God, Jesus, the church and the world. It grows immediately out of his most central theological concerns. *The church is the renewed family of God, in the **Messiah** and in the power of the **spirit***; and its family life must reflect that fact. Just because we in the modern West live in nuclear families with (for most of us) rather small contact with our fellow Christians, certainly by comparison with the early church, that shouldn't blind us to the reality of the extended Christian family that Paul was dealing with.

Christian theology, then, is closely bound up with guidelines for healthy family living. We don't have to read very far between the lines of this passage to see where unhealthy ways of organizing the extended family might creep in, and where strong guidelines need to be provided. Three words lurk behind the passage, giving us the clue to what's going on: power, sex and money.

Power: those entrusted with responsibility in the church need to learn how to use it with gentleness and wisdom. There will come a time when the pastor needs to tell individuals that their thinking or behaviour is out of line. This is, and ought to be, very, very difficult; I suspect that people who find it easy are a danger to themselves and others. Those in authority are often tempted to lord it over others, to come down on them from a great height. This must be resisted. Think how you might go to your own beloved father and tell him, gently but clearly, that something has got to change. That's how to approach an older man. If it's someone younger, think how you would speak to your own brothers. And the same with women (obviously if Timothy had been a woman Paul might have said this bit the other way round): think about your mother and your sister. The little phrase 'with all purity', added at the end of verse 2, indicates that Paul is aware of a potential problem when the intimacy of pastoral relationships generates sexual attraction. Pastors must be scrupulously careful at this point. Failure here causes not only scandal and heartbreak; it can poison the atmosphere of an entire community.

Money: the problem of how to help widows includes the problem of who is really to count as a widow. In a community where many entire households had become Christians, there was no point enrolling a widow for church support when she still had children or grandchildren able to help. It doesn't take much imagination to see the resentment that would cause. Paul has harsh words for those who neglect their own family responsibilities (verse 8), and almost equally harsh ones for those who, while being technically widows (possibly at quite a young age; many people in those days died in their twenties and thirties), were living off the church's support while having extra help from their families, and could thus afford a life of lazy leisure. If the self-giving love of God in Jesus ends up enabling people to be self-indulgent, something has gone badly wrong somewhere.

The crucial question – and it's just as crucial in the twenty-first century as in the first – is how we join together the family life of all God's people and our responsibilities within our own families. This calls for imagination and flexibility within the clear guidelines laid down here. We need to watch out for the traps and dangers, for the abuse of power, sex and money, and to hammer out in each generation what it means to live as the family of God.

1 TIMOTHY 5.9–16

Widows

[9]Let a woman be registered as a widow if she is at least sixty years old, the wife of one husband, [10]with a reputation for good works, having brought up children, shown hospitality, washed the feet of God's people, helped those who were suffering, and been steadfast in doing good wherever she can. [11]Refuse to register younger widows. When their desires become strong against the Messiah, you see, they will want to marry, [12]and they will receive condemnation because they have abandoned their earlier faith. [13]In addition, they learn the habit of idleness, going around from one house to another, not only wasting their time but gossiping and meddling, saying things they shouldn't.

[14]So this is my wish: the younger ones should marry, have children, run their households and give the enemy no opportunity to slander us ([15]some, you see, have already gone off after the satan!). [16]If any believing woman has relatives who are widowed, let her help them, so that the church won't be burdened. That way, it can help widows who really are widows.

I like the old joke about the two different types of people. You can divide the world into two: those who think there are two types of people and those who disagree.

But there really are two types when it comes to establishing a new community. There are the dreamers and the doers, and we need them both. You have to have people who glimpse a vision of how it all could be different. You have to have people who ask the awkward questions like, 'Where's the money coming from?' 'How are we going to heat this place anyway?' and 'Where are we going to build two extra toilets?' Dreamers tend to get exasperated with doers: fancy worrying about those details when we're creating utopia! Doers tend to get fed up with dreamers: head in the clouds, romantic, unpractical! If the enterprise is to succeed, they need each other and have to learn to get along.

Very occasionally you find someone who bucks the trend and combines the two roles into one. I think Paul was like that. He could dream, no question about it; his glorious, soaring vision of God's people as already seated with the **Messiah** in **heaven** is nothing if not utopian. But he could get things done as well. Look at the way the two come together in 1 Corinthians – the visionary and the practical flowing smoothly into one another. And there's plenty of both in this letter as well.

But people often come to the Bible expecting only dreams. They want a big picture in which the glorious vision of God's new world is held out before them. If there have to be rules, they want large, general commands which will apply to all kinds of circumstances. If you start getting down into what people call 'case law' – what happens in this situation, what to do if faced by that problem, and so on – they get bored or even exasperated. That wasn't what they wanted.

That's often the reaction to a passage like the present one. This is a 'doer' passage, and many of us find dreams easier to handle. What's more, most people who read the Bible are not responsible for organizing a community which looks after widows, so they are tempted to glance at a paragraph like this, frown and pass rapidly on.

In addition, some people who've read this passage in the last generation or so get angry with it. How dare the writer, they think, pontificate about what age a woman should be before she gets help from the church? Isn't it rather arbitrary? And, in particular, what right has he got to tell young widows that they should marry again? Isn't that the sort of personal choice they should be free to make for themselves?

Most of these objections have to meet the obvious point: this passage is written by someone who had been doing his best to organize actual communities, and had discovered that the grand ideas needed bringing down to earth. What might ideally have been the case – wouldn't it be nice (we might think) if all those in any kind of need could be supported generously by church funds – doesn't match up with the reality. The church is often quite poor and has to make hard decisions about where to draw lines. Sometimes those decisions will seem arbitrary, just as someone who dreams of a wonderful, beautifully decorated home must eventually decide whether their favourite picture should hang on this wall or that one. If you wait to discover an abstract rule for deciding every detail, you will wait a very long time, and meanwhile there are things to be done and people in urgent need of help.

So the present passage, continuing the previous one in its attempt to see how best to help widows, reflects four obvious problems which the early church must have faced. Thinking about these will help us to see how the passage can then relate to other situations as well, including some we may face in our own day.

First, Paul insists in verses 9 and 10 that widows enrolled on the church's support list must be above a certain age, and must have shown by a lifetime of family and community service that they are bona fide recipients of the church's generosity. A moment's thought will reveal what would happen otherwise. Just as nineteenth-century missionaries had to cope with the problem of 'rice Christians' (people who professed conversion in order to get food), so it would have been easy for widows on the edge of the church's life to try to sign on both at a younger age and without having shown by their previous life that they were, through and through, active family members of the church in their own right. Of course, we would want to protest, the church should err on the side of generosity. But, as those who administer charitable monies today know only too well, with limited funds available the church should emphatically not be taken for a ride by those who are out for a free and easy time. Converts of convenience are not to be tolerated when it comes to solid practical support.

Second, Paul is clear that those who can be supported by other means should make that their first priority. He's already insisted that a widow's own relatives should be her first line of support; now he warns (in verses 11–13) that enrolling widows too young can lead to the bad situation where, having begun to accept the church's generosity and live within its common life, they suddenly decide to throw it over again; or, finding themselves provided for but with no domestic duties, they get into bad habits and become centres of discontent or disruption. Paul clearly sees being enrolled as a widow as a commitment to make the Christian community one's primary family, something few of us (outside monastic communities) have ever even thought of. He's aware, as all such communities soon realize, that there are tensions and dangers which must be noted and avoided, preferably before they become urgent.

Third, he therefore counsels that younger widows should marry again. Unusually for him, he says this is a 'wish' (verse 14); perhaps he means 'this isn't a rule, but it's what I like to see happening, and here's why'. His reason is that the non-Christian world, looking on at this strange experiment in community living that calls itself the Messiah's people, the King's family, will be only too eager to find causes to sneer and mock. 'Oh,' they will say, 'I see, you've organized a nice little extended family with all these attractive young widows just sitting around all day . . .', and the innuendo will turn into gleeful pointing of the finger when one of the young widows does indeed go off and get married, particularly if it's to a non-Christian. I don't read these verses, then, as a high-handed command to women about how to organize their personal lives. I see them as a warning to the community that, if it intends to take seriously the project of living as a mutually supportive family, there will once more be serious problems to face and avoid.

Fourth, he insists again, as in the previous passage, that Christians must care for their own family members in the first instance. It's interesting that he places this burden on Christian *women* specifically in verse 16. I suspect this, too, is a way of outflanking an obvious danger. Supposing a married Christian man sees a widowed female relative in need, and goes to her aid. How easy it could be, within that relationship, for inappropriate emotions to be aroused. That danger needs to be avoided before it happens.

Those who give professional help and counsel to people in positions of responsibility and authority will see, I think, that this passage was written by someone with enormous experience of community life and its problems. We do well not to dismiss it out of hand because it isn't the kind of thing we normally expect in the Bible. And we do well to examine our own communities with the same degree of wisdom and sensitivity to pitfalls and dangers.

1 TIMOTHY 5.17–25

Elders

[17]Elders who are good leaders ought to be paid double, particularly those who work hard in speaking and teaching. [18]The Bible says, you see, 'Don't muzzle an ox when it's threshing', and 'the worker deserves his pay'.

[19]Don't accept an accusation against an elder, unless it is supported 'by two or three witnesses'. [20]When people persist in sin, rebuke them openly, so that the rest may be afraid.

[21]Before God, Messiah Jesus and the chosen angels, I give you solemn warning to keep these commands without discrimination. Never act out of favouritism. [22]Don't be too quick to lay hands on anyone; don't share in other people's sins. Keep yourself pure.

[23]You should stop confining yourself to drinking water. Use wine (in moderation!). That will be good for your digestion, and for the physical problems you often have.

[24]Some people's sins are obvious, and walk ahead of them into the courtroom. Other people's follow them there. [25]In the same way, good works are obvious; but, even when they aren't, they can't stay hidden for ever.

I had an urgent message the other day from a friend. He is a priest, and was applying for a new job in a different country. The trouble is that he has family responsibilities, and after doing all the calculations he reckoned he simply couldn't live on the stipend offered by the parish that wanted to take him on. What should he do?

All I could advise was realism. I wanted to say 'if it's right, the Lord will provide', and we both believe that to be true. But part of deciding whether it's right is deciding whether you can meet your obligations, or whether you are going to be forced either into extra work on the side or into failing in some of your primary responsibilities.

I was brought up, of course – as I suppose we all were in my country fifty years ago – to believe that it was important *not* to pay clergy very much, in case they were tempted to go into the job in order to earn a 'good' salary. This has resulted in the bizarre situation where even a junior member of the clergy in the United States of America earns as much as a bishop in England, and only the Archbishop of Canterbury himself earns as much, in England, as the average parish minister in America. Of course, both of them would seem fabulously wealthy to the great majority of Christians, who, living in Africa, Asia and Latin America, where entire countries are struggling to pay off massive and unjust debts, find it hard even to survive. This is the daily reality of many churches, and that's where we should begin our thinking on this subject.

But into this thorny set of problems we find verses 17 and 18 declaring – to a Christian community that was composed, most likely, of poor people – that elders who give good leadership, or who work hard at preaching and teaching, should be paid double. (Some translations say 'double honour', but the word most naturally refers in this passage to money, not social respect.) And the command is backed up with two quotations, one about oxen not being muzzled while they're working hard, and one (which looks like a biblical quotation but is actually a reference to Jesus' own teaching) about workers deserving their pay. Once again, this part of the letter is quite close to 1 Corinthians, in this case 9.3–11.

Double pay for good leaders and teachers! That's not something you hear too often in parishes and church committees, and I can imagine enormous resentment if anyone tried to put it into practice. After all, who's to decide whether this or that person is really 'good at leading', or is working especially hard at teaching and preaching? I can see in my mind's eye endless committees being set up to review different applicants, and the whole thing becoming an embarrassing waste of time.

Yet there is an important principle at stake. The churches in much of the Western world – and by 'churches' I basically mean the non-ordained people, who form the great majority of members and give the great majority of such money as there is – have allowed themselves over the years to slide by, insisting that of course the clergy shouldn't earn as much as other people, without noticing that now most clergy spouses, in Britain at least, find themselves forced to work to help the family budget; that clergy have fallen not only way behind people with similar professional qualifications, but also behind those with none; and that though (thank God) there are still plenty of people willing to make the enormous **sacrifice** to give up a lucrative career elsewhere in order to preach the **gospel** and look after God's people, there must be many others who, with major family commitments, simply cannot afford to do so. There are serious questions here for the churches to address in the next generation – not least how to talk about money without sounding as if they simply want to get rich themselves.

This passage moves quickly from one topic to another, but the second point, in verses 19 and 20, continues with instructions about the way elders (or 'presbyters' – that's the word in Greek, referring to the senior office-holders) should be treated. It will happen from time to time, alas, that members of the congregation have something of which they wish to accuse office-holders. Often enough, human nature being what it is, this arises from jealousy or other unworthy motives, and so, if only one person is making the accusation, it should not be accepted. (It's easy enough to think of circumstances where only one person would be in a position to make the accusation, but that's the trouble with legislating for particular circumstances; as soon as you try to list all possibilities, you end up writing a very large book.) Paul reaches for the biblical commandment that accusations should only be accepted if two or three witnesses agree. Again, we all know that witnesses can agree to lie; but this is only the first stage of proceedings, when the charge is admitted and needs hearing.

Timothy, it seems, is to act in all this as a senior elder – pretty much the role that became known as 'bishop'. This emerges even more clearly in the next pair of verses (22 and 23), where Paul recognizes that there will be enormous pressure on Timothy to act favourably towards the people he likes. To see what this pressure would be like in practice, just imagine the hurt look on the face of a dear friend when you tell them they are out of line. Leaders cannot allow themselves to slacken on this point. Likewise, though there will be plenty of people who Timothy will think should be brought forward as newly appointed ministers of the gospel, he should go slowly at this point. It's easy, in a fit of enthusiasm, to ordain someone; but it's tragic, when it becomes clear that the person wasn't ready, to have to discipline them afterwards. It may turn out that, by being party to the process of their ordination, you have appeared to connive at things they have done in the past. The church has been in deep trouble in recent years for turning a blind eye, over a long period of time, to wicked behaviour among its clergy, and the next generation must take steps to avoid repeating the same mistake. A slow process of character evaluation will pay dividends (verses 24 and 25).

Into this set of instructions, Paul inserts a comment to Timothy, urging him to relax what appears to be a self-imposed rule against drinking wine (verse 23). Medical tests today confirm that, for most adults, regular wine in moderation is good for the digestion, the heart and several other parts of the body. Paul has noticed that Timothy is a stern self-disciplinarian, who has perhaps learnt that even a little too much alcohol impairs judgment, speech and behaviour, and so has decided to avoid it altogether. But he has also noticed that Timothy is subject to regular health problems which might actually be improved by moderate doses of wine. Once again, this letter avoids the heights and flights of theological rhetoric, but gives us down-to-earth, practical wisdom. The church needs both. Woe betide us when we exchange high theology for the spirit of the age, and practical wisdom for the kind of shoulder-shrugging, do-your-own-thing advice of so many modern moralists.

1 TIMOTHY 6.1–5

Slaves, Masters and Sound Teaching

[1]All who live as slaves, 'under the yoke' so to speak, should consider their own masters as worthy of all respect, so that people may not say wicked things against the name of God and the teaching. [2]Those who have masters who are also believers should not look down on them because they are brothers, but rather give them service, since those who receive the benefit of their work are beloved fellow believers.

Teach these things, and exhort people to do them. [3]Some people teach other things, and don't hold firmly to the healthy words of our Lord Messiah Jesus, and the teaching which goes with piety; [4]people like that are conceited and have no understanding. They have a diseased craving for disputes and arguments about words. That just leads to envy, jealousy, evil speaking, wicked suspicions [5]and irritating arguments among people with depraved minds who have lost their grip on the truth and imagine that godliness is a means of gain.

Supposing the world goes on for another thousand years and the Christians alive at that time look back at our generation, what will shock them most?

We could each, no doubt, draw up our list of (other people's) failings and faults, and, by projecting our dislikes onto the future, declare that this or that will be deemed outrageous. Some will highlight the way in which white Christians went along with the oppression of their black brothers and sisters; others will focus on the massive problem of debt in the Third World. Some will declare that Western Christianity has lost the plot entirely when it comes to sexual morality; others, no doubt, will imagine that a thousand years from now Christians will be comfortable accepting a wide variety of sexual practices as normal. And – who knows? – it may be that among the things future generations will regard as scandalous about our present behaviour will be our unthinking use of oil-based products as a major energy source. We are polluting our planet day and night, burning up resources and making a great mess. And our nuclear alternatives aren't much better. 'After all,' people may say, 'they had the wind and the tides, the waterfalls and the sunshine, and the technology to harness them – why didn't they use them?' And we might not have any good answers. We might find ourselves ashamed of the way we took our energy sources for granted and never asked awkward questions about them.

As we look back at the first century, and ask, 'Why did they seem to tolerate that?', one of the biggest things that worries us about the early Christians – as, indeed, the ancient world in general – is their main energy source. And that, of course, was slavery.

You only have to press the button marked 'slavery' to provoke a strong negative reaction. We all know it's wrong – though there are, in fact, many forms of virtual slavery around the world today, where people cannot escape dead-end, low-paid jobs or make them more bearable. We all value 'freedom', though we don't always know exactly what it is, how it works, or what to do to maintain it. And because the only thing we have to say about slavery is 'it's wrong', we cannot believe that the early Christians didn't have the same reaction.

The answer is, of course, that many of them did. But in Paul's day slaves formed up to one-third of the population. Most free families except the very poor owned at least one or two. Declaring grandly that you were opposed to the whole system would achieve about as much as someone today standing up in church and announcing that they were opposed to the use of oil-based products and therefore regarded cars, planes and motorized boats as unchristian. What the early Christians did, with Paul at their head, was to declare that masters and slaves were in fact equal before God (Galatians 3.28), and to treat both alike as possessing individual responsibility before God. What's more, in this passage he has thought his way forward from this general principle to the consequent situation and the problems it poses. As in Romans 13, he was anxious that the little Christian communities shouldn't get a name for pointlessly provocative and disruptive behaviour, and that Christian slaves with Christian masters should work at their strange new relationship in a wise and mutually respectful fashion. Of course, we wish it hadn't taken so long for the Christian world to abolish slavery; and now, if we know our business, we should wish that we hadn't been so quick to invent new forms of it. What we can hardly do is quarrel with the practical wisdom that gave usable Christian advice to real people in real situations rather than formulating abstract principles which would make the moralist feel good but which would be no use to the human beings concerned.

Verses 3 to 5 sound as though they were written by someone with long experience of dealing with what we sometimes call 'the awkward squad'. They are like people who, faced with well-cooked, healthy food, are always grumbling that the diet doesn't suit them, that they would prefer something lighter, or something more solid, or whatever. The basic **gospel** teaching, and the guidelines for the complex and delicate business of organizing a Christian community which is more than just a churchgoing club, are wholesome, and good for people; but there will always be some who don't like it, and who have become conceited and incapable of understanding what's going on. Things often end up in wrangling and arguing about the meaning of particular words – something scholars have to do, of course, in order to understand ancient texts, but not something that ought to become the main element of Christian discourse. Where that kind of squabble becomes the norm, the community breaks down into factions, as people stop trusting one another and imagine that everyone else is stealing a march on them.

It's not a happy picture. And yet it's a familiar one. The antidote Paul is offering isn't the one most people today would ask for, either. Today, in the Western world at least, people who sense a dispute on the horizon may be tempted to shrug their shoulders and walk away. Paul saw the answer as being clear, firm, Christian leadership, with solid teaching backed up by exhortation.

There is one more worrying element in the picture of the grumblers. It appears that somewhere near the heart of the problem is a desire to make money from Christianity, as though the more devout you were the more you might get out of it. Perhaps some imagined that they could set themselves up as teachers and hawk the new religion around the world the way some ancient philosophers and other teachers used to do. Paul will have more to say about this in the next paragraph. But what we have here is enough to show that, once clear teaching and exhortation starts to fail, we can expect nothing but trouble. Other agendas will come in to take its place. And when that happens the careful work of building up a community of love, trust and witness will be undone in a flash. It can happen today. We must make sure it doesn't.

1 TIMOTHY 6.6–10

Godliness and Contentment

⁶If it's gain you want, though, there is plenty to be had in godliness – if it's combined with contentment. ⁷We brought nothing into the world, after all, and we certainly can't take anything out. ⁸If we have food and clothing, we should be satisfied with it. ⁹People who want to be rich, by contrast, fall into temptation and a trap, into many foolish and

> dangerous lusts which drown people in devastation and destruction. [10]The love of money, you see, is the root of all evil. Some people have been so eager to get rich that they have wandered away from the faith and have impaled themselves painfully in several ways.

It is hardly an exaggeration to say that this famous passage is an indictment of modern Western culture. Never before in history has there been such a restless pursuit of riches, by more and more highly developed means. Never before has the love of money been elevated to the highest and greatest good, so that if someone asks you, 'Why did you do that?' and you responded, 'Because I could make more money that way', that would be the end of the conversation. Never before have so many people tripped over one another in their eagerness to get rich and thereby impaled themselves on the consequences of their own greed.

The greatest irony of it all is that it's done in the name of contentment – or, which is more or less the same thing, happiness. Many people give lip service to the maxim that 'money can't buy you happiness', but most give life-service to the hope that it just might, after all. 'The pursuit of happiness', and the idea that this is a basic human right, is all very well, but when it's taken to mean the unfettered pursuit of wealth it turns into a basic human wrong. And yet every advertisement, every other television programme, many movies and most political manifestos are designed, by subtle and not-so-subtle ways, to make us say, 'If only I had just a bit more money, then I would be content.' Nelson Rockefeller, one of the richest men of his day, is reputed to have summed it up. When asked by a reporter how much money he reckoned he needed to live on comfortably, he replied, 'A little more than I get'. Most of us, from the quite poor to the very rich, would be tempted to say 'Amen' to that.

We all know the counter-argument, though it doesn't do much (granted the continual cultural bombardment) for our mental stability on the subject. If you make a lot of money, you might want to buy more houses and more wonderful things to put in them; whereupon you multiply the risk of burglary, so you get more expensive burglar alarms and insurance policies, and you end up employing people to look after you and your property. So you need to make more money again, and for that you will need to hire accountants, and probably lawyers too, not to mention investment advisors and stockbrokers. And meanwhile the monkey on your shoulder is whispering that maybe you should try this scheme to get a bit richer ... and then this one ... and now what about this ... if only you had a bit more, you could relax and be content. But in fact the only way to contentment is to sack the monkey and be content with what you have.

Of course, there are plenty of people in the world who live on or below the actual poverty line. For them, earning a little more really would make the difference between sheer misery and at least the chance of contentment. But, usually, they don't suffer much from the love of money. They are not staying up half the night devising more and more complicated ways of multiplying their wealth. Getting a job, or a slightly better job, will do the trick. Then the real things in life – food, family, house, clothes – will follow.

This paragraph, with its solid (though to us difficult) wisdom, combines well with the teaching about food and sex at the beginning of chapter 4. The point is that the present world, the created order in which we live, is full of all kinds of good things. We should enjoy them in their appropriate ways, and, by thanking God for them, maintain the careful balance of neither worshipping the created world nor imagining that it's evil. But when money comes into the equation everything looks different. Money is not, as it stands, God's creation, but a human invention to make the exchange of goods easier and more flexible. The further it becomes removed from the goods themselves, and the more it becomes a 'good' in itself, the closer we come to idolatry. A society which values wealth for its own sake – which is where the Western world has been for at least the last few decades – has forgotten something vital about being human. Money itself isn't evil; but, as verse 10 famously puts it, loving money is not only evil, it's the root of all evils.

People sometimes challenge that analysis. The rapist doesn't attack out of love for money. The sadistic torturer wants to cause pain and would actually pay for the privilege of doing so. But even with sex and power, money isn't far away. Many rapists have had their appetites titillated by a culture which has soaked us in sex in order to get us to part with our money. Many who have fallen in love with firearms, weapons and all the accoutrements of a life of violence, have gone that way because someone was eager to make money out of them. And, at the international scale, we can see only too easily how it works. Industrial giants give huge donations to a political party. When the party gets into power, it awards its friends huge contracts. Often these include, or even focus upon, the manufacture of arms. Why do we need arms? Why, to fight a war, of course. And so we go looking for one, not primarily to do justice in the world but to feed the monkey on the shoulder. And this time we impale not only ourselves, but also many others, on the bayonets and lances of our own greed.

It's a sorry picture. But in the background stands Paul saying '*There is a different way*'. We don't have to live like that. What's more, the church is called to model the different way. Do we have the courage to try? If so, the next passage could be the most significant advice our culture, and we within it, have heard for a long time.

1 TIMOTHY 6.11–16

The King's Royal Appearing

> [11]But you, man of God – you must run away from all this. Instead, chase after justice, godliness, faith, love, patience and gentleness. [12]Fight the noble fight of the faith, get a firm grasp on the life of the coming age, the life you were called to when you made the noble public profession before many witnesses. [13]I give you this charge before God, who gives life to all things, and Messiah Jesus, who made the noble profession before Pontius Pilate: [14]be undefiled and blameless as you keep the commandment, until the royal appearing of our Lord Messiah Jesus, [15]which the blessed and only Sovereign One, the King of kings and Lord of lords, will reveal at its proper time. [16]He is the only one who possesses immortality; he lives in unapproachable light; no human being has seen him, or can see him. To him be eternal honour and power, Amen!

As I write this, London is getting ready for another major royal event. It is the fiftieth anniversary of the Coronation of Queen Elizabeth II, and the crowds and the television cameras are taking up positions to celebrate the day with a big service, special music and great banquets. Whatever people think of monarchy in general and this monarch in particular, there is no question that this will be a spectacular day. When the queen emerges from Westminster Abbey after the service, flags will wave, bells will ring, crowds will cheer. People who witness it will remember it, most likely, for the rest of their lives.

The first-century world, without the benefit of television, knew how to organize great royal displays so that the emperor's appearance would be stunning and spectacular, giving the onlookers something to remember for a long time. Since a fair part of the empire already worshipped the emperor as divine, or at least 'son of god' (the 'god' in question being the previous emperor), the idea of his 'appearing' combined the two notions: a major spectacular state visit, and a moment of divine revelation. The word which summed all this up was *epiphaneia*, the word from which Christians get 'Epiphany'. That's the word Paul uses in verse 14, the word I've translated 'royal appearing'. He is deliberately talking about the future 'appearing' of Jesus in language his hearers would recognize as normally belonging to Caesar, the Roman emperor.

Anyone writing this and anyone reading this, at any time during the first century within the Roman world would know just how subversive it was. But it isn't just a hint. Paul rubs it in, line after line. When you follow King Jesus you are enlisting in the service of the One True God, the King of kings and Lord of lords, the ultimate sovereign. All earthly monarchs must bow before him. The 'appearing' of his son is the only royal 'appearing' that will ultimately count.

But if Paul is taking on the claims of Rome in this passage, he is also taking on the claims of Greek philosophy – claims which a good many people, including many Christians, continue to believe to this day. Many philosophers ancient and modern have believed that each human being automatically possesses an immortal '**soul**', an inner, non-physical **life** which will live on after bodily death no matter what they do. Indeed, many people have tried to state a would-be Christian doctrine of salvation in these terms, with the most important question being what will happen to this 'soul' in the afterlife. Paul challenges this head on. He does indeed believe in an afterlife for all people, and in a judgment at or after death which will determine the happiness or misery of the life to come. That is clear from many passages in his writings, for instance Romans 2.1–16. But he never states this in terms of people having an immortal soul, for the very good reason that he doesn't believe it. *Only God possesses immortality* (verse 16). God is the ultimate reality: his very being consists of such blinding light that the brightest human illumination is dark by comparison, and must hide from his dazzling brightness. Where human beings gain a new, deathless life (that's what 'immortality' means), they do so because he gives it to them as a fresh gift of grace (see, for instance, 1 Corinthians 15.52). And for Paul this new, deathless life won't be lived as a disembodied soul. It will be lived as a new, risen body. In a few clear, sharp, celebratory sentences Paul has taken on the power of Rome and the wisdom of Greece with the essentially Jewish challenge of the **gospel** of Jesus.

This way of looking at the passage gives a special flavour and power to the commands that come at the beginning. It's all too easy for us to read verses like 11 ('justice, godliness, **faith**, love, patience and gentleness') and 14 ('undefiled and blameless') and to think, 'Yes, well, he's telling me I must learn to behave better.' That's true, of course, but the point of it all is that these are the ways you must get in shape both to be ready for the King when he appears and to enlist in his service during the present time. The emperor would summon people to fight in his army, and when they signed on for military service they would have to make a public declaration of their allegiance to him. Now Jesus is summoning people to fight in *his* army – though this battle is not one that involves weapons and killing, but love, patience and gentleness. It is 'the noble battle'.

The word 'noble', which Paul seems to have on the brain in verses 12 and 13, can mean 'good' or 'beautiful'. It's one of the highest praise words available in his language. When you sign on for this noble struggle, you make 'the noble public profession', the baptismal declaration that Jesus is Lord. You are reminded of Jesus himself, standing before Caesar's representative, Pontius Pilate, and declaring that he was indeed the King of the Jews, in other words, the **Messiah**, the world's true Lord. The commands in verses 11 and 14 are not just about learning to behave in new ways for their own sake. They are the essential requirements for effective soldiers in the army of the true King.

This whole way of life forms a stunning contrast with the attitude described in the previous passage (those who want to be rich, who fall into traps and impale themselves on sharp objects). It encourages us to lift up our heads and see where we're called to go, rather than looking around at the rest of the world and being consumed with jealousy for the material wealth that others have got.

This contrast is embodied in the vigorous language Paul uses to describe how we should avoid that sort of lifestyle and embrace the way of Jesus. Think of an animal you'd really be afraid of, whether it's an angry rhinoceros or a large spider. If you came round a corner and found yourself facing it, what would you want to do? Run away, of course. Well, that's how you should feel about the greedy, jealous lifestyle of those who want to be rich. Then think how you'd feel if you saw the person you loved best in all the world, who you hadn't seen for years, walking down the street. What would you do? Why, chase after them, of course. Well, that's how you should behave with these virtues: justice, godliness, faith, love, patience and gentleness. They don't come about by accident. They occur in someone's life because that person has chased after them energetically, has worked at them, has chosen again and again to live that way rather than the other way. People who do that discover in the process that they are beginning, in the present, to live 'the life of the coming age' (verse 12). That's why, when the King of kings reveals his son, they will be ready for him and will celebrate his royal appearing.

1 TIMOTHY 6.17–21

What to Do with Money

¹⁷What about people who are rich in this present world? Tell them not to think of themselves too highly, and to set their hopes, not on something so uncertain as riches, but on the God who richly provides us with everything to enjoy. ¹⁸They are to do good, to be rich in good

works, generous and eager to share. ¹⁹That way, they will treasure up for themselves a good foundation for the future, and thereby come to possess the life which really is life.

²⁰Well then, Timothy: keep guard over what has been entrusted to you. Turn away from the pointless and empty talk and contradictions of what is wrongly called 'knowledge'. ²¹Some have claimed to be experts in it, but have missed the target when it comes to the faith.

Grace be with you all.

'We'd have been all right if it hadn't been for the stock market crash.'

He was a delightful man, full of kindness and fun, looking back on a long and exciting life. He had travelled widely, met lots of interesting people, written books, climbed mountains and brought up a large family. He had been looking forward to a happy retirement in the large old house his family had lived in for generations.

And then it happened. Most of his savings had been tied up in investments. He'd followed the best advice. He'd checked the credentials of the companies where the money was invested. But overnight the markets around the world had fallen through the floor, and he and millions of others discovered that their substantial savings were almost worthless. Now he couldn't afford to keep up the house, and he was having to move somewhere much smaller.

Many people who read this may be tempted to feel jealous that anyone should have had that kind of money in the first place. I'm aware of that temptation myself! We need, perhaps, to go back to verses 9, 10 and 11 for a minute. Part of the point of the present passage, highlighted in verse 17, is *the uncertainty of riches*. Not only can't you take it with you when you go, as verse 7 reminded us, but you can't be sure you're going to keep it while you're here. In a world increasingly dominated by money it seems almost indecent to mention it, but the New Testament, as so often, is severely practical, and reminds us of facts our culture wants us to forget. Money comes and goes; God doesn't. Money can't be relied upon, and even those who have plenty of it discover all too soon that it doesn't buy them contentment (back, again, to verse 8). If you have trained yourself only to get enjoyment from things that cost money, you need to go into a different sort of training.

Paul does not, however, tell people with money that they must give it all away at once. Jesus once told someone to do that (Mark 10.17–22), because he could see that in his case wealth was the idol that was keeping him enslaved and stopping him following the call of God's **kingdom**. There are, no doubt, many people in that condition. Jesus frequently reminded his hearers of the danger. But there are others who, for whatever reason, happen to have more money than their basic needs require, and who need wise instruction on what to do with it. Here it is.

To begin with, they are not to use their money to give themselves airs. An arrogant aristocracy, ruling by an accident of birth, is bad enough; an arrogant plutocracy is even worse. Rather, those with more money than they need (and 'need' doesn't mean 'want'!) must find appropriate ways of doing good with it. There was a time when people with money built schools and hospitals, or even churches. There was a time when the rich became patrons of the arts; many works of lasting beauty, whether paintings, symphonies or whatever, exist because a rich patron was prepared to back a poor but talented artist or composer. Often a particular project that may be enormously worthwhile in itself needs some initial start-up money, and a gift from a wise patron can set something in motion which can then run itself and do good for many years to come. And as those with money discover the joy of enabling new things to come into being, so they will become, deep down, 'generous and eager to share'. It won't be a grudging 'Oh, all right then'. It will flow from the heart. I know one or two people like that, and they are the kind of people nobody would be jealous of, because their overflowing generosity is so appealing.

What about the promise of verse 19, that people who are generous with their material wealth will 'treasure up a good foundation for the future'? Does that not imply that they are using their money to buy their way into God's new world? Not at all. The New Testament is clear from start to finish that the eventual goal of our pilgrimage will be in accordance with the life we have led. We are assured of that goal from the very start, from the moment we come to **faith**; that is part of what 'justification by faith' is all about. But then, because God's **spirit** is at work within us, we are commanded to live our lives in accordance with the new world we have already entered by faith. When we reach the goal, the risen and glorious **life** in God's new world, we will discover that the life we have led in the spirit, in obedience to God, is indeed preparing and shaping us for that new world.

This is so whatever our circumstances. If we are poor, our required obedience will be appropriate for our poverty. If we are rich, our required obedience will be appropriate for our wealthy state – and it may mean giving it all away. The point in either case is not that one category has an unfair advantage, but that each, like artists in training, must carve their own statue from the block of marble they've been given, not from the next person's. The end in view is 'the life which really is life', as opposed to the life of the **present age**, which is a bare shadow of that which is to come.

The letter ends, abruptly it seems to us, with a warning about something not mentioned before in this letter. From later Christian writers we hear more details about a movement which, from small beginnings in Paul's day, grew to a major force in the second and third centuries. It took many forms, and often borrowed the language of Christianity, even attempting to enlist Jesus as an early teacher of its doctrines (through selective quotations from, and adaptations of, his sayings). This movement believed in a special kind of 'knowledge'. At its heart this meant the secret or hidden knowledge that you were, yourself, one of the few special people, a spark of light imprisoned in a body but called to be free of it. The Greek word for 'knowledge' is *gnosis*, and the movement became known as 'gnosticism'. It was characterized not least by endless speculations about what this spark of light really was, and the various levels of spiritual beings whose multi-layered **heaven** it was supposed to inhabit. When you find yourself following this sort of path, Paul is saying, you know you're on the wrong track. 'The faith' – genuine faith in God as the good creator of a good world, and in Jesus as the beginning of the new creation – leads in an entirely different direction.

The contemporary Western world has seen the rise of new forms of 'gnosticism'. Many people today long to believe that they possess a hidden identity, long covered up by their outward body and circumstances. Many then believe that true life consists in being true to this hidden identity at all costs. Some even try to make out that this is Christian teaching. It wasn't, and it isn't. Jesus calls us now, as he called his first followers, to accept his offer of new life, not to discover a secret one we already have. To put it another way, he calls us to 'find our lives by losing them'. And the life that we find will be the **resurrection** life in God's newly recreated world.

It is perhaps because of the robustly physical nature of God's creation, and God's new creation, that we find throughout this letter so much attention to the practical details of organizing the church into a healthy community. That, it seems, is how God's grace is to work out in practice, the grace which Paul's closing greeting wishes upon Timothy and those with him. Grace doesn't ignore the concrete and specific problems and challenges. Like Jesus himself, it comes down to the practical level, gets its hands dirty, and gets on with the job. That's what we should expect, after all, from a genuinely 'pastoral' letter.

2 TIMOTHY

2 TIMOTHY 1.1–7

Rekindle the Gift!

[1]Paul, an apostle of Messiah Jesus by God's will, according to the promise of life in Messiah Jesus; [2]to Timothy, my dear child. Grace, mercy and peace from God the father and Messiah Jesus our Lord.

[3]I serve God with a clear conscience, as my forebears did, and I am grateful to him that I remember you all the time, as I pray for you night and day. [4]I remember how you cried when I left, and I'm longing to see you and be filled with joy. [5]I have in my mind a clear picture of your sincere faith – the faith which first lived in Lois your grandmother and Eunice your mother, and which, I am confident, lives in you as well.

[6]That's why I now want to remind you that God gave you a gift when I laid my hands on you, and that you must bring it back into a blazing fire! [7]After all, the spirit given to us by God isn't a fearful spirit; it's a spirit of power, love and prudence.

There was snow outside, and the living room was cold when I came downstairs. I don't know why I'd woken up early, but I now shivered as I huddled on the sofa and waited for one of my parents to follow me downstairs. (I can't have been more than about seven or eight, I suppose.) Before long my father appeared, and began to work on the fireplace. He twisted some newspaper, laid some fresh sticks, placed coal around the edge, and then, kneeling down, blew very gently at the base of the fire. He didn't need to use a match. He'd seen that the coal in the very bottom of the fireplace was still glowing, still just alight. As he blew, I watched in amazement at what seemed like magic. The coal glowed brighter and brighter, and then suddenly the newspaper burst into flame. Within a minute the sticks were alight, the fire was going, and the room began to warm up.

A small childhood memory of the days before central heating. But I'm reminded of it when I hear Paul urging his young friend to rekindle God's gift, to bring it back into a blazing fire. Something is glowing there, deep down inside Timothy, and he must blow gently on it to bring it back into flame.

We want to know, of course, what this 'gift' was. Was it a special kind of speech? Prophetic utterance, perhaps, or tongues? Was it the ability to interpret scripture and teach God's **word** with power? Was it the authority and ability to lead a congregation? I suspect, putting two and two together, that it was some combination of the latter two. The first letter warned Timothy not to let other people look down on him because he was young (1 Timothy 4.12). Paul urges the Corinthians not to regard Timothy as junior and inferior (1 Corinthians 16.10–11).

Now he tells him that the **spirit** which is at work within him, God's spirit given to equip him for service, is not a spirit of fearfulness or timidity, but a spirit of power, love and prudence. If Timothy is to be true to his calling he must learn to act with all three of these qualities.

First, power. People are suspicious of power, quite rightly. We've all heard the famous saying that 'power tends to corrupt, and absolute power corrupts absolutely'. Power can be bad for those who exercise it, as much, if not more, as for those over whom it is exercised. And yet power is inevitable and necessary within human relationships. Someone has to make decisions. Someone has to protect the weak and vulnerable. Someone has to regulate the common life of a complex society. Someone has to give other people a sense of direction. This is just as true in the church as it is in the world around. We are not solitary individuals living out our lives in detached isolation. Anarchy doesn't enable people to flourish either as humans or as Christians. The New Testament insists that God intends human authorities to bring order and harmony to the world.

This is just as true of the church as it is of society as a whole. God gives some people gifts to be used for the benefit of all; among these is the power to make things happen within the life of the church. This power is mysterious. It isn't simply a matter of holding a particular office on the one hand, or of having a forceful personality on the other; by themselves, both of those can become dangerous. It's a matter of having the ability to do and say things which change situations, to give a lead which others find that they want to follow, to speak words of wisdom which prove compelling, and to bring healing and hope where it's most needed.

Timothy, clearly, has been given gifts in this direction. Precisely because he appears not to have a particularly forceful personality, he needs to be encouraged to use these gifts without being afraid. As he does so, he must also act with love. Power divorced from love quickly becomes destructive, if not even demonic. Love without power can degenerate into wishy-washy sentimentality. But when the person who is exercising power is known and perceived to be someone whose whole direction of life is generous, self-giving love, people are naturally more inclined to follow the lead they give, and obey their instructions. The power of the **gospel** itself flows from the fact that God gave his own son for our sake, thereby establishing a claim on our answering love and loyalty. Ministers of the gospel must discover that same power and love in their own work.

The spirit who pours out this love and power also gives Christian leaders prudence. They must be able to think clearly and shrewdly about what needs to be done and how best to do it. This must naturally begin with their own lives, where they learn moderation and self-discipline; but it will also apply to their ordering of life in the community of God's people. We do not, alas, need very much experience of common life in Christian circles to see how easily self-promotion, jealousy, petty rivalries and so on can spring up. Leaders at every level urgently need prudence, as well as power and love, so that they may be able to look back without regret at decisions taken and attitudes adopted in their personal life as well as in their leading of the church.

This still doesn't tell us what gifts Timothy had been given, which he is now to stir up and rekindle. But it strongly suggests that they had to do with leading the young church, giving it wise teaching and direction.

Paul can urge him to do this with confidence because he knows that Timothy is securely rooted in the **faith** itself. They had worked closely together (we see another account of this in Philippians 2.19–24), and Paul knows that his faith is deep-rooted, going back to some of the earliest influences on his life, the witness and example of his mother and grandmother. Lois and Eunice must have become Christians very early on, since Timothy himself was already a Christian by the time Paul met him on his second missionary journey (Acts 16.1). What's more, Paul and Timothy had had a close personal and working relationship, like a father with a son (in a world where sons were often apprenticed to their fathers, working alongside them and learning by watching as much as by listening). So close had they been that, when the time came for Paul to move on, Timothy had been moved to tears. As we read verse 4 we can feel how much that had affected Paul as well.

But of course the deepest roots of all that Paul is beginning to say lie in God: God's will, God's promise (verse 1), God's grace, mercy and peace (verse 2), God's gift of colleagues and friends (verse 3). Paul never acts or writes simply out of personal whim. His life is rooted in grateful prayer, standing in the millennia-old tradition of Jewish prayer to the one true God. It is out of that prayer that he writes to Timothy. This letter is not simply a comment on what God has done and is doing; it is designed to be, itself, a part of that work. May it be so for us, too.

2 TIMOTHY 1.8–14

Don't Be Ashamed!

⁸So don't be ashamed of the testimony of our Lord, nor of me as his prisoner. Rather, suffer for the gospel along with us, in accordance with God's power. ⁹God saved us, and called us with a holy calling, not according to our works, but according to his own purpose and grace.

He gave us this grace in Messiah Jesus before all time and ages, [10]but has now made it visible through the appearing of our saviour Messiah Jesus, who abolished death and, through the gospel, shone a bright light on life and immortality.

[11]I was made a herald, apostle and teacher for this gospel; [12]that's why I suffer these things. But I am not ashamed, because I know the one I have trusted, and I'm convinced that he has the power to keep safe until that day what I have entrusted to him.

[13]Keep a firm hold on the pattern of healthy teaching which you heard from me, in the faith and love which are in Messiah Jesus. [14]You have had something very important entrusted to you, too; make sure you look after it, through the holy spirit who dwells in us.

My grandfather was a clergyman, and like many of us who have to stand up and do things in front of other people he had a recurring nightmare. In his dream, he would find himself standing in the pulpit getting ready to preach a sermon, and look down to discover that instead of clerical robes he was wearing pyjamas. Or perhaps underwear. (I don't have that dream; instead, I often dream that I'm arriving at the church after the service has already started, and that my robes and sermon are locked in the boot of the car and I can't get them out.) What the dream is telling us is of course that, deep down, we are afraid of being ashamed in public. There are many different levels of shame, but even at an informal social level most of us feel a stab of shame if we turn up at a party dressed differently to everyone else. We have our hidden codes and assumptions. You wouldn't go to the beach as though dressed for a grand concert, or vice versa.

Paul's world had a highly developed set of codes for honour and shame, and everyone knew how they worked. There were all kinds of things that would bring shame on a person, or a family, or a city. Many of them related to their visible status in relation to the power structures of the day. In our own time, someone who has been on holiday with the president or prime minister may well discover that they have thereby acquired honour, respect, admiration or jealousy in the eyes of others. Someone who is clearly out of favour with the ruling circles may discover that they are cold-shouldered. This works further down the scale as well, as people who claim acquaintance with celebrities (rock stars, fashion models, sports heroes and the like) acquire a kind of honour.

In Paul's world, there was a carefully graded system of social power and prestige. Those who were in some way associated with, or friends of, those who had this power could hold their heads up and expect preferential treatment in the shops and businesses of the town. Those who were out of favour with the rulers could expect that ordinary people in the street would sneer at them as well.

No prizes, then, for guessing where Paul came within these social scales. He was in prison! That spoke for itself, as it would do today, even if we know that some people have been put there unjustly. There is still a stigma attached to imprisonment. It robs a human being of something fundamental, the freedom to come and go, to make their own decisions and live their own life. They are belittled in all kinds of ways. In Paul's case, anyone who knew why he was in prison would have no difficulty in seeing the point. The reason he was there was that what he had been doing and saying was seen as an offence to the people in power. He was announcing a royal message, a '**gospel**' which clashed head on with the royal message on which the Roman empire was built: the announcement of Caesar as Lord, the promise of his power to save the world, the prospect of his royal appearance in a city or province that obeyed his rule. 'Paul in prison' meant 'Paul out of favour with the power brokers of the day'.

Paul knows, then, that even his friends and colleagues may feel under pressure to distance themselves from him, to be ashamed of him – and so, in effect, to be ashamed of the gospel of King Jesus. Even Timothy may be tempted to give in to this pressure. The antidote to this temptation is to recognize and celebrate all the more the power Paul spoke of in the previous passage – God's power, brought to light through the **resurrection** of Jesus (verse 10). God's power overrides all earthly power. It has already been put to work in the call of the gospel which has transformed Paul's and Timothy's own lives and is doing so for an increasing number of others as well (verse 9). It will be put to work again when God makes the world anew and gives his people new **life**, new bodies, thus fulfilling the promise of life for which his people trust him in the present (verse 12). This is the main theme of the passage: that if Timothy really understands the nature of God's power, he will learn to line up his sense of true honour and shame in relation to God himself, instead of in relation to the fickle, shifting and at best secondary earthly powers. And Paul uses his own life and work (verses 11 and 12) as the model for Timothy to copy (verses 8 to 10).

Let's take the underlying sequence of thought step by step. The heart of it all is what Paul says in verse 10: God has revealed 'our saviour, King Jesus'. The 'appearing' of Jesus contrasts with the shabby, pretentious 'appearing' of Caesar, however grand his royal robes, however powerful his armies. Jesus' status as the world's true saviour contrasts with the claims of Caesar to be the rescuer, the deliverer, of the world (all tyrants and conquerors claim that they are 'saving' or 'liberating' people from something or someone). And the event above all which has revealed Jesus in this way is his resurrection – not because he has been the subject of some bizarre **miracle**, but because death, the regular final weapon of Caesar and all tyrants, has thereby been defeated. As a result, something had been brought to light which even the best pagan imagination could only dream of: a life that had gone through death and come out the other side into a new existence beyond the power of death. This was an 'immortality' far superior to the kind imagined by the great pagan philosophers. Some of them (Plato, for instance) believed that each human being possessed an immortal **soul** which would survive bodily death. The kind of immortality offered by the gospel is a new bodily life which will not be subject to pain, sickness or death.

This new life, though, isn't something all humans possess automatically. It is a gift of God in sheer grace and power; and it is rooted in something that happens to people during this present life. That's the point of verse 9. When the gospel is preached, when King Jesus is proclaimed, people are summoned to believe, trust and obey God rather than anyone or anything else. That's what Paul means by 'calling'. This happens not because we're special, or because we've behaved in a particular way up to now, but simply by God's goodness and love. When you realize what the Christian gospel is all about – the resurrection of Jesus as the unveiling of God's power, and the call of God to you here and now, putting that power to work in your own life, bringing the promise of your own resurrection in due course – then your entire world of values is turned upside down. You will be ashamed of some of the things you were formerly proud of, and proud of some things which previously would have made you ashamed. That is what Paul wants to happen to Timothy.

As, indeed, it has happened to him, to Paul himself. He is the gospel's royal herald, and that's why he's in prison and suffers many other things too. But his own trust has always been in God's power. Part of that trust is that he has committed himself, his own life and work, to God, and he knows that God will keep safe what he has committed to him (verse 12).

This leads to a final twist in the line of thought. Christians commit themselves to God, like someone putting their most precious possession into safekeeping in a bank or secure vault. But at the same time God commits something to us: a particular calling, a new set of responsibilities, and ultimately the new life itself, the life we have in the present through the **spirit**. Our task is to be faithful and responsible before God, as he is utterly faithful and reliable for us. Along that path lies the kind of life which will never be ashamed, in whichever direction the winds of fashion, political fortune and popular opinion may blow.

2 TIMOTHY 1.15–18

Foes and Friends

> [15]You will know that everyone in Asia has turned away from me, including Phygelus and Hermogenes. [16]May the Lord give mercy to the household of Onesiphorus; he has often refreshed me. He wasn't ashamed of my chains, [17]but when he was in Rome he eagerly hunted for me and found me. [18]May the Lord grant him to find mercy from the Lord on that day. And you know very well all the things he did for me in Ephesus.

The most difficult thing I have found in Christian ministry is opposition from people I thought were friends, or at least colleagues, fellow-workers. One of the hardest parts, of course, is the nagging thought that people who disagree with me might be right, and that they are finding it just as awkward as I am to come to terms with the fact that *I* am disagreeing with *them* and opposing their ideas, plans and dreams. Whenever we find ourselves confronted by someone who disagrees with us, we need to remind ourselves that they probably feel that we are confronting them.

This humility, which is normally necessary and healthy, doesn't always apply. When the Confessing Church in Germany in the 1930s stood up to Adolf Hitler in the name of Jesus **Christ**, there wasn't room to say, as we should in day-to-day disagreements, 'Well, you may be right; let's go away and think about it some more.' The Confessing Church simply had to say, to Hitler and those in the churches who supported him, 'No: you are wrong, you are leading people astray from God's way.' The same was true, as we now see, with those who were opposing apartheid in South Africa in the second half of the twentieth century. There wasn't room for anyone to say 'Well, some of us think black and coloured people are different and inferior, and some of us think all people are equal in the eyes of God; let's agree to differ.' We now see that shrugging our shoulders on issues like that was intolerable. At the time, however, many people were anxious about taking a hard-line stance, especially when it carried serious political, social and personal consequences.

We need to remind ourselves of this when we are tempted, as we surely often are, to find Paul a bit too hard-edged, a bit (as we say) dogmatic. How, we ask, can he say, 'Everyone in Asia has turned away from me'? If we met a church leader who said, 'I used to work in Manchester, but everybody there now disagrees with me', it would sound strange; we might ask ourselves whether it wasn't the leader himself who had such strange ideas that nobody in their right mind would agree with him. But this is what Paul is saying about 'everyone in Asia'. (Asia, we should remind ourselves, was the western part of modern Turkey, with Ephesus among its chief cities.)

At one level, Paul must have felt a colossal failure. He had spent a lot of time in the province of Asia, particularly in Ephesus. He had preached the **gospel** to them, taught them, lived alongside them, wept and laughed and prayed with them. They had been dear to him and he to them. And now he says they've turned away from him. What does he mean?

He probably doesn't mean that they have rejected Jesus, or come to disbelieve in the basic Christian **message** he had preached to them. The evidence of churches in Asia after Paul's day is clear, not least in the book of Revelation. But he may mean that the cutting edge of the gospel, as he saw it, had lost. The Asian Christians may perhaps have come to accept what the rival teachers had been saying in Galatia some years before: that Jewish Christians and **Gentile** Christians belonged in different categories, and ultimately at different tables. As we know from Paul's letter to Galatia, he saw that as a failure to understand the meaning of Jesus' death. Or perhaps they had turned his message about Jesus as the true saviour and Lord, and hence the one before whom Caesar is shown up as an impostor, into the more comfortable belief that Jesus was offering a private religious experience which wouldn't bring you into direct confrontation with the principalities and powers. He would certainly have seen that as a betrayal.

Or perhaps the problem was less theological and more practical. Perhaps they had heard that Paul was in prison in Rome, and had decided to make it clear that they weren't anything to do with him, in case they became tarred with the same brush. (This would then be parallel to Paul's complaint in 4.17, that when his case first came to court nobody stood up for him.) And maybe the sign of this is that they had stopped sending financial support to Paul. People in jail in the first century were not provided for by the state. They were entirely dependent on friends and family to bring them the basic necessities of life. Paul had been relying on his friends from Asia to keep in touch and look after him.

In particular, he had been hoping that Phygelus and Hermogenes would remain loyal supporters. This is the only reference to them anywhere in early Christian writings, so we don't know any more about them than what we can glean by reading between the lines at this point; but what we find tells a sad story. It must have been disappointing and distressing for Paul – something that Christian leaders today do well to remind themselves when they are tempted to see the early **apostles** as 'successes' and themselves as 'failures'. But along with the sorrow there went (as so often) a wonderful encouragement. One person had stood out as a shining example. Onesiphorus and his household had come to the rescue and stood by Paul.

Onesiphorus, too, is only known to us from this passage. But, again, this reference tells a large and impressive story. We know three things about Onesiphorus from verses 16, 17 and 18, and each of them is instructive as we think about Christian work in our own day and especially about those who get into trouble for preaching the gospel.

To begin with, Onesiphorus did what Paul was urging Timothy to do a few verses ago: he was 'not ashamed' of Paul as a prisoner. That, actually, is putting it mildly. 'Not being ashamed' might sound to us as though he simply thought about him kindly from time to time; but Onesiphorus didn't just think, he acted. He was prepared to be associated with Paul, to search for him, and to look after him. He wasn't frightened of being known as a friend and colleague of someone with a reputation for being socially, politically and religiously subversive. This gives us a further clue as to what Paul was really hinting earlier when he told Timothy not to be ashamed of him. He wanted him, too, to come and see him (4.9, 21), to be with him, to be prepared to be identified with him, however dangerous it might seem.

What was more, Onesiphorus didn't just happen to stumble upon Paul and decide that he might as well do something for him. He took the initiative, sought him out and found him. He had been with Paul in Ephesus, which may imply that he wasn't himself originally from Rome; but, undeterred by a new and unfamiliar city and surroundings, he got on, made enquiries and tracked Paul down. As so often, we are here frustrated because we would like to know when precisely this imprisonment took place, and we don't. Acts ends with Paul under house arrest, but not, it seems, chained up. He was able to receive visitors and entertain them. Our present passage sounds much worse than that. It seems as though this may be a second imprisonment, following a 'first hearing' which went badly wrong (4.16). Different people have proposed different theories. What matters here, though, is not reconstructing the history but noting the behaviour. There is all the difference in the world between coming by accident on someone in need and making a sustained and eager effort to find them and help them.

Thirdly, Onesiphorus' help was severely practical. No doubt Paul enjoyed simply having him there; but when he says that he 'refreshed' him I think he means quite literally that he brought him food and drink, and perhaps money to buy more after he had gone. We can't all do this kind of thing, but probably a lot more of us could than presently do.

There is one more thing, of course, to say about Onesiphorus, and about what Paul thinks of him. Paul prays that he may 'find mercy from the Lord on that day', the 'day' in question being of course the 'day of the Lord', the day of the final 'appearing' of Jesus as saviour and king. Paul clearly thinks that Onesiphorus' final salvation will be in accordance with the love and mercy he has shown. This doesn't mean that Onesiphorus, or anybody else, 'earns' their ultimate salvation by a relentless programme of unaided moral good works. Salvation, and the **justification** which anticipates it in the present, remain a free gift. But when God's **spirit** is at work in someone's life, enabling them to live here and now the life of generous, Christlike love, there we see a true anticipation of their final reward.

2 TIMOTHY 2.1–7

Conditions of Service

[1]So, then, my child: you must be strong in the grace which is in Messiah Jesus. [2]You heard the teaching I gave in public; pass it on to faithful people who will be capable of instructing others as well. [3]Take your share of suffering as one of Messiah Jesus' good soldiers. [4]No one who serves in the army gets embroiled in civilian activities, since they want to please the officer who enlisted them. [5]If you take part in athletic events, you don't win the crown unless you compete according to the rules. [6]The farmer who does the work deserves the first share of the crops. [7]Think about what I say; the Lord will give you understanding in everything.

When I was at school, I shared a study for several terms with a friend. We got to know one another very well, the way you do when you find yourself in the same room, studying, meeting people, making coffee, snoozing over difficult tasks, worrying – or perhaps fantasizing – about the future, and so on.

I dread to think what stories he could tell about me, and I could respond in kind. But one thing we both noticed about the other: we were both, at one stage, past masters at putting off as long as we could the daunting task of writing an essay. I would always know when he had difficult work to do: he would cut his nails, tidy his desk, rearrange his record collection and even sweep the floor. Anything to stave off for another moment, and then another, the challenge of creative thought and writing. Most of us, faced with a task we know will be demanding and difficult, find ways of avoiding it, even though we know we can't put it off for ever.

Paul is warning Timothy against any such avoidance tactics when it comes to the central challenge of witnessing to the royal **gospel** of

Jesus in the face of social and political stigma and danger. He must take his share of suffering, as one of the King's good soldiers. As in 1 Timothy 6, Paul is drawing on an obvious image from the Roman empire: you could tell when you were under the emperor's rule when there were Roman soldiers ordering you about or threatening to punish you if you didn't obey instructions. The soldiers of King Jesus, of course, are on a different mission and under totally different orders. Indeed, part of the difference is precisely that Caesar's soldiers characteristically inflict suffering on others, while Jesus' troops receive it themselves for loyalty to their crucified Lord. But they, like Caesar's men, have to be ready to obey their sovereign at once, without stopping to think, without any avoidance strategies.

Paul uses three overlapping images, in verses 4, 5 and 6, to show what he means. He begins (not surprisingly, since he's been talking about Christians as 'soldiers of King Jesus') with a point about life in the army. If a soldier wants to please his commanding officer, and so be in line for better pay or promotion, he will concentrate on military tasks. He won't spend time in the life of the local community, as though he really were a civilian after all. There is a life of discipline and obedience, focused on certain key operations, and the soldier mustn't get distracted or sidetracked. In the same way the Christian, called into cheerful confrontation with the world that resists the gospel, mustn't look for easier activities on the side which would keep him or her busy but not embody the cutting edge and challenge of the gospel.

The second picture, as often in Paul, is from athletic games, which were popular throughout the Roman world, often in connection with major religious or imperial festivals. If you want to take part in an athletic competition, there are rules to be observed: you must do what the race officials tell you, you must follow the track and not cut corners, your discus or javelin must be of the proper kind, and so on. There are equivalent things to be said about living and working as a Christian, and Paul will say some of them in the rest of this letter. But for the moment he is mainly concentrating on the challenge: don't take the easy way out! Don't look for a loophole, a shortcut, a way of seeming to win the event while in fact cheating. (The day I was writing this, a newspaper article appeared with stories of people competing in a marathon and taking a cab for part of the way.) It's all too easy for some people to imagine that because they are now Christians they can take whatever easy way through they choose; they're going to be saved anyway, so why bother? Paul would regard that in the same way that an athlete who had trained hard, and was competing flat out, would regard someone who, without training or effort, sneaked across the stadium and claimed victory without breaking into a sweat.

The third image is from farming. Often, in both the ancient and modern worlds, the main labourers on a farm would be tenants but the landlord would own the crop – and might not give the actual workers more than a small share in it. Paul appeals to a kind of natural law, a universal folk wisdom: the one who does the work deserves the first share of the produce. The point here is clear. Beware of the temptation to engage in the Christian life like a kind of absentee landlord, expecting the benefits without having to do any of the hard work. By the same token, if you want rewards, get on with the work.

And the nature of the work is clear: suffering. Western Christians have often found it hard to come to terms with this. It was assumed for a long time that most if not all people in Western countries were practising Christians; people supposed, therefore, that there would be no clash between religious and civil duty. In the last two hundred years or so the picture has changed; people now assume that religion is about private spirituality and salvation, and thus they imagine that it won't impinge on public affairs to the point where others will be angry and persecute religious believers. But for Paul and Timothy Christianity is about following King Jesus, which requires all the strength that his generous grace can give (verse 1). In particular, it will involve standing out for the gospel, the royal announcement, even when it challenges the assumptions and practices of the world – and the empire – all around. It is perhaps one of the greatest challenges facing Christians today to see what the contemporary equivalent of all this might be. This is where we, like Timothy, need Paul's urgent command to think over what he's saying (verse 7); mull it over, try to explain it to yourself and others, generate some discussion in your church about it. As you do this, trust that the Lord will give you understanding.

Part of that understanding will come as we, like Timothy, think carefully through the apostolic teaching and make sure it gets passed on, in one piece and in good order, to those who come after us (verse 2). This concern for continuity, for safe transmission of teaching, has sometimes been seen as a boring, conservative traditionalism, as though by simply saying the same thing, generation after generation, people would somehow be enlivened by the gospel. This is of course a caricature. The gospel which must be handed on is the most revolutionary **message** ever heard. Not passing it on intact doesn't mean that the next generation is free, spontaneous and able to do its own thing, but that the next generation can quietly trim off the awkward bits, the challenging elements, the features that will make them stand out and get into trouble. Handing on the tradition safely is the only way to make sure that the next generation, too, is summoned, whatever it costs, to follow the radical gospel of King Jesus.

2 TIMOTHY 2.8–13

God's Word Is Not Tied Up

⁸Remember Jesus the Messiah, risen from the dead, from the seed of David, according to my gospel – ⁹for which I suffer like a criminal, even being chained up! But God's word is not tied up. ¹⁰That's why I put up with everything for the sake of God's chosen ones, so that they too may obtain, with glory that lasts for ever, the salvation which is in Messiah Jesus. ¹¹You can rely on this saying:

If we die with him, we shall live with him;
¹²if we endure patiently, we shall reign with him;
if we deny him, he will deny us;
¹³if we are faithless, he remains faithful,
for he cannot deny his own self.

'Sticks and stones may break my bones,' goes the old rhyme, 'but calling names won't hurt me.' It may be good to mutter little jingles like that if people are being rude to you, but actually the rhyme is only partly true. And when it comes to Christian witness in a hostile world, we are called to believe that the power of words, and the power of God's **word** in particular, is greater than the power of prison walls and chains of iron.

Faced with outright hostility to the **gospel** message from the powers that be – they could see clearly enough, what many modern Christians ignore, that to announce the crucified and risen Jesus as the world's true Lord was to offend against the all-powerful claims of Caesar – Paul reached deep into the Jewish traditions for the theology that sustained him, and could also sustain Timothy and other younger Christians as they watched his example and wondered if they had the courage to follow it. One of the great themes of Isaiah, in the middle section of the book (chapters 40—55), is the living and abiding power of God's word:

All flesh is grass,
And all its glory is like flowers in a field;
Grass withers, flowers fade . . .
But the word of our God endures for ever. (40.6–8)

As the rain and snow come down from heaven,
And don't go back there, but water the earth,
Making it bring forth and sprout, giving seed to
sowers and bread to eaters,
So shall my word be, that goes out of my mouth:
It won't come back to me empty,

But it will do what I plan, and succeed in the task
for which I sent it. (55.10–11)

God's word is the thing that will sustain the Israelites as they face
exile and oppression in Babylon. At the heart of the long section of
Isaiah flanked by these two great statements of trust we find the picture of the royal, anointed servant of the Lord, who will accomplish
in himself the salvation which God promises, through his words, but
ultimately through his obedient suffering. This is exactly what we find
in the present passage.

Paul's 'gospel', in fact (verse 8), is not a religious system, not even a
message about how people may be saved (though it includes that on
the way). At its heart it is the announcement that Jesus is the king, the
anointed one, the Lord of the world, a claim which would be astonishing and unbelievable were it not for the fact that God raised him from
the dead. The message which centres upon him, which proclaims him
as Lord to a surprised and often angry world, is 'God's word' indeed,
the word which God has entrusted to **apostles**, preachers and teachers,
the word which sums up the entire Bible of the day (the Old Testament) by speaking of Jesus as the fulfilment of God's age-old plan.

Just as, for Isaiah, confidence in God's word was meant to sustain
God's people when they were suffering, to give them fresh courage and
hope when the pagan world was oppressing them, so it is with Paul. This
passage continues his encouragement to Timothy, his insistence that he
must be prepared to face whatever suffering may come his way in the
course of announcing and living out the gospel of Jesus. Timothy must
remind himself constantly that it is indeed Jesus he is announcing and
following – Jesus, who faced the might of Rome and remained faithful
to death, and whose **resurrection** demonstrated that he wasn't just a
member of David's family, the Israelite royal house, but that he was the
true 'seed of David'. Paul says something very similar in Romans 1.3–4.
And Timothy may well find, like Paul, that if he is faithful to this message he will end up in trouble, in prison, wearing a chain like a common
criminal.

But, just as in Philippians 1.12–18, Paul isn't going to let his imprisonment dampen his spirits, or his **faith**. I may be tied up, he says, but
God's word isn't tied up! Far from it; in fact, when people try to sup-
press the true claims of the gospel, that's the sure sign that it's doing its
work, that it's making inroads into people's minds, into their imagination, into the way they find themselves called to live. And that means
that Paul is prepared to put up with whatever suffering comes his way.
He does it (as he says in 2 Corinthians 4.7–15) for the sake of all God's
people. It is as though he is drawing the enemy fire on to himself, to

2 TIMOTHY 2.8–13   God's Word Is Not Tied Up

create a breathing space in which the young church can grow and develop, can become strong in faith and hope. He has his eye not on the **present age**, but on the new world that is to come, the coming time when all God's people will not only be saved from their present plight but, more particularly, receive glory.

What is this 'glory'? People sometimes talk as if it will mean shining like a light bulb – as though there were, ultimately, anything particularly splendid about that. In God's eyes, a human being, reflecting his image and likeness, is more important than the brightest star in the sky. True, some passages in the New Testament do speak of Jesus and his people shining like stars (an idea which appears first in Daniel 12.3). But the 'glory' of which Paul and the other New Testament writers speak has more to do with the status, the role, which God's people will be given. In verse 12, as in passages like Romans 5.17, Paul talks about 'reigning' with **Christ**. God's new world will not simply be a place of rest and refreshment, as people often imagine. That's what awaits God's faithful people immediately after death; but after that again, when God brings the new creation into existence, there will be new work to do, new tasks to stretch our ability and imagination. Those who are faithful in the present world will be given authority in the next one, where they will share Jesus' reign.

So, like the jingle with which we began, though this time rooted in the reality of the gospel, Paul passes on to Timothy an early Christian proverb. It's the sort of thing you can imagine people learning by heart, teaching to their children and friends, and then repeating under their breath when standing before tribunals, when being threatened by angry magistrates or beaten by guards, when facing sudden and fierce temptation:

If we suffer, we shall live,
If we're patient, we shall reign;
Deny him, he'll deny you;
If we're faithless, he is faithful,
For he can't deny himself.

There is, of course, a surface-level peculiarity about the third and fourth lines of this little jingle. Jesus himself did warn that he would deny before his father those who denied him before other people (Matthew 10.33; Mark 8.38). This remains as an awful warning, turned into a terrifying and dramatic scene in the **parables**: 'I do not know you,' says the bridegroom to the girls who fell asleep (Matthew 25.12; compare Matthew 7.23). But alongside even this denial, the most terrible words I can imagine ever being spoken to me, there is a further promise. 'If we are faithless, he remains faithful.' This abiding faithfulness is, according to the saying, rooted in Jesus' own character: 'He can't deny himself.' How can we resolve this? Is Paul saying in one line that denying Jesus brings terrible consequences and in the next that it doesn't after all?

No. I don't think 'faithless' here means 'if we lose our faith', in the sense of ceasing to believe that Jesus is Lord and that God raised him from the dead. I think this is meant to take account of the fact that our faithfulness – our reliability, our stickability, our resolve, our determination to remain 'faithful' in the sense of 'loyal' – will waver and wobble from time to time. Those under intense pressure, whether political, spiritual, moral or whatever, will sometimes find themselves weak, faint and helpless. It is at those times that they need to learn a kind of second-order faith, a faith in the utter faithfulness and reliability of God himself, the God we know in and through Jesus, who was himself faithful to death. There is a world of difference between being blown off the ship's deck by a hurricane and voluntarily diving into the sea to avoid having to stay at the helm.

2 TIMOTHY 2.14–19

Foolish Words and the Word of Truth

> [14]Remind them about these things; and warn them, in God's presence, not to quarrel about words. This doesn't do any good; instead, it threatens to ruin people who listen to it. [15]Do your very best to present yourself before God as one who has passed the test – a workman who has no need to be ashamed, who can carve out a straight path for the word of truth. [16]Avoid pointless and empty chatter. It will push people further and further towards ungodliness, [17]and their talk will spread like a cancer. I'm thinking in particular of Hymenaeus and Philetus; [18]they have turned aside from the truth by saying that the resurrection has already happened. They are upsetting some people's faith. [19]But God's firm foundation stands, and it has this as its seal: 'The Lord knows those who belong to him', and 'Everyone who uses the name of the Lord must leave wickedness behind.'

'What we need to know', said the young lawyer, 'is what Professor Johnson really means by "reform". He says he's proposing a "reform" in the way we admit undergraduates to the College. But the word "reform" really means "the same thing in a new form". What he's offering us isn't the same thing at all. It looks to me much more like a "replacement". He wants to abolish what we've always done and do it totally differently. He might as well have said "revolution". And that's never been our style in this College. We have never liked' (he paused for effect, and emphasized the last word) 'revolutionaries.'

The Master, chairing the meeting, sighed deeply. He knew what was going on. Most of the Fellows of the College had been in favour of the new proposal. It had been carefully thought through, studied in detail, and was designed to make real and substantial improvements in the system. But there were two or three who opposed all change as a matter of principle; and clearly they had put up this young teacher of law to cast a spell of words, not about the proposal itself, but about the way they were proceeding. By playing with the words 'reform', 'replacement' and 'revolution' he was able to sow doubt in the minds of several colleagues who had been happy to follow the argument but now might feel obliged to vote against it. They didn't want to think of themselves as revolutionaries. The vote was taken. Several voted against. Others abstained. The proposal was lost by a narrow margin.

Playing with words has always been a favourite game of politicians, lawyers and (alas) theologians. As I have often said before, it is of course necessary to study words and what they mean. Part of the discipline of Bible study involves dictionaries and concordances; we need to check, as carefully as we can, that we really have understood what the words, the sentences and the passages actually mean, as opposed to what we might imagine they mean, or were once told that they mean, or might want them to mean. But that task, which is essentially humble, open to being taught, is completely different from the way in which some people crack a whip like a circus ringmaster and make words dance on their hind legs and do things they were never meant to do. I received a letter only the other day – a long, rambling discourse – from someone who was determined to persuade me that '**resurrection**' was really the same thing as 'reincarnation'. On and on went the argument, turning and twisting words and meanings this way and that. I can imagine that many people, not familiar with the details of what the two words have meant over the years, might have found it quite convincing. Yet it was rubbish from beginning to end.

Resurrection is, in fact, one of the topics about which Paul has spotted foolish talk already beginning to creep in to the church. Two people – whether they are official teachers or not he doesn't say – have begun to teach a novel idea: that 'resurrection' refers to something which has already happened, rather than the glorious future, the new embodiment, which awaits all God's people at the last day.

We can see, perhaps, how this happened. Paul himself spoke of Christians, in **baptism**, dying and rising with Christ (Romans 6). He declared boldly that there is a sense in which Christ's people have already been raised with him, and have indeed taken their seat with him in the **heaven**ly places (Colossians 3.1–4). But, as Romans and Colossians both insist (not to mention Paul's other letters), this does *not* mean there isn't still a future, bodily resurrection. What happens is that through baptism and **faith** the Christian *anticipates* that final event, and must learn to live by faith and hope in the present on the basis of what's promised in the future. But then, it seems, some Christians began to wonder. Could they really believe in a *bodily* resurrection – either for themselves or even for Jesus? Surely that was taking things a bit too far? Didn't it fly in the face of all scientific evidence? (They knew plenty about that then; we didn't have to wait for the eighteenth century to discover that dead people stay dead!) So they tried to adjust the Christian **message**. It wasn't, they suggested, really about anything so crude as an actual resurrection in the future. It was about a spiritual experience in the present, leading to a disembodied eternal bliss. Nothing more.

This line of thought became popular in some circles about a hundred years after Paul, and has had a good run again in our own day. But it goes completely against everything Paul believed. It denies the goodness of the physical creation, and the promise of God to renew it. It denies the ultimate justice of God, and his promise to put the world to rights. It puts the focus not on God, the **gospel** and the world, but on me and my spiritual experience. And it leads – as the more developed writings of the second century show in abundance – to endless speculations, quarrels about words, and pointless and empty wranglings. It brings us, in fact, back to where we began. When we start this kind of playing with words and ideas we should regard it as a danger sign. It may well mean that we are drifting away from the solid gospel itself.

Over against such things, Paul offers a portrait of the Christian 'workman', the one who knows how to study scripture and how to preach and teach God's **word**. Such a person, particularly a young person in training like Timothy (though, God knows, all of us preachers and teachers are still in training), must think of their work as if they were an apprentice coming up to a qualifying examination. 'Present yourself before God as one who has passed the test' (verse 15): in other words, figure out what standards of knowledge, expository skill, historical and literary judgment, and above all spiritual understanding, are required for the job, and make sure you possess them. Then you will be 'a workman who has no need to be ashamed'.

When we moved into our present house, two carpenters built the new bookcases I needed. I once built a bookcase myself, and, being unskilled, made an awful mess of it. Within a few years it had collapsed, and I broke it up for firewood. I am ashamed of my own efforts in that department. But these two carpenters were real professionals. I remember the day they stood back and looked at their finished work.

No need to be ashamed. These bookcases would do the job for many years to come. What's more, they looked great. That's the kind of effect Paul wants us to strive for in our understanding and teaching of scripture and the gospel.

In particular, he wants preachers and teachers to 'carve out a straight path for the word of truth'. Some translations say things like 'rightly dividing the word', and it's possible Paul means something like that (in other words, 'being able to show how the sentences work, what each part means, and how they all relate to each other'). But it's more likely that the picture he has in mind is of a pioneer hacking out a path through the jungle so that people can walk safely through. Part of the job of the teacher is to do what Paul himself is doing in this passage: to see where there are brambles, creepers and dead trees blocking the path which the word should be following to people's hearts and minds, and to shift them out of the way.

Instead of all the speculation, Paul gives straightforward, almost proverbial, rules of thumb which anyone can get hold of. These are part of the firm foundation that all Christians should be prepared to build on. Faced with uncertainty about who we really are – the uncertainty which gripped many in the ancient world as it does in our own day – we can rely on God's knowledge of us. Faced with moral chaos, which was likewise a feature of Paul's world as much as ours, we can get our bearings from straightforward commandments. If we are going to take the Lord's name on our lips, and claim him as *our* Lord, then we have no choice but to leave behind, however painful it may be, all kinds of wickedness and injustice. No need to wrangle about words. Just a clear commandment, a clear promise and a clear call to God's people to stand firm.

2 TIMOTHY 2.20–26

Vessels for God's Use

[20]In a great house there are vessels not only of gold and silver, but also of wood and pottery. Some of them are given special honour in the way they're used; others are for menial purposes. [21]So if people purify themselves from dishonourable things, they will become vessels for honour, made holy, pleasing to the master of the house, fit for every good work.
[22]Run away from the passions of youth. Instead, chase after justice, faith, love and peace, along with all who call on the Lord from a pure heart. [23]Avoid silly and unprofitable disputes, because you know that they produce fights; [24]and the Lord's servant mustn't be a fighter, but must be gentle to all people, able to teach, able to bear evil without

resentment, [25]able to correct opponents with a meek spirit. It may be that God will give them repentance so that they can arrive at a knowledge of the truth, [26]and, in coming to their senses, escape the devil's snare, after having been held captive by him and made to do his will.

My wife and I are about to move house again. We've done it quite often enough already, but I have a new job to go to, and there it is. And so, once more, we've had to think about all the things we own – the clutter of old china and furniture, as well as one or two nicer things which we've been given from time to time. I have been reminded of the wise old saying that you should only have in your house things which you know to be useful or believe to be beautiful. I suspect that, if we applied that criterion strictly, there would be at least one load of rubbish to be thrown out. We shall see.

Paul's mind is moving, in the illustration he uses at the beginning of this passage, between two different though related ideas about the sorts of objects people have in their houses. Some china, glass, silver and maybe even gold is beautiful and valuable; you keep it for special occasions. Other bits and pieces are more for everyday use, and you might keep them out of sight if you had special guests coming, though there is nothing wrong or embarrassing with them in themselves. But Paul seems also to be thinking about a different sort of object – the old rag you use to mop the floor, the shovel you use to tidy up after your dog, and so on. These actually have 'dishonourable' uses. When he applies the idea to human beings, stretching the point perhaps, it doesn't just mean not having any usable skills or gifts. It means abusing or dishonouring your own self, making it good for nothing, treating yourself as something worthless. Paul seems to be suggesting that sometimes humans take objects (their own selves, their own bodies) which are meant for honourable use, and use them for purposes which bring them shame.

There are two ways in particular in which people dishonour themselves, and Paul regularly comes back to them (compare, for instance, Colossians 3.5–8). There is sexual misconduct on the one hand, allowing your desire for physical and emotional gratification to lead you into patterns of behaviour which downgrade and devalue one of God's great gifts. And there is anger and bitterness, in which, even if your cause is perfectly just, you do it no favours by expressing it in ways which hurt and further alienate those you are trying to convince.

Paul's way with the first of these is not, in this case, to spend long on analysis, but to encourage Timothy to run: to run away from anything which would lead him into sexual self-indulgence of the kind particularly powerful among young men, and instead to 'chase after' the powerful virtues of justice, **faith**, love and peace. As he lives and works with the community of God's people he will find that together they can work at these large but infinitely worthwhile pursuits. But when he comes to the second, to the question of anger, he goes into more detail, teaching Timothy important lessons about how to be a pastor when faced with people who oppose and argue.

Young clergy in particular often find this a difficult lesson to learn. You study hard for two, three, maybe even four years. Perhaps you do a doctorate, in biblical studies, pastoral psychology or whatever. You attend innumerable training days, study weekends, practical work-shops. Finally, after what seems half your life in preparation, you are launched on a parish or community. And one of the first things that happens is that someone who hasn't had any of your training, who has never studied the subject at all, and who hasn't even thought of it before he heard your first sermon, tells you to your face that you're wrong.

Your natural tendency will be to feel professional pride. You know what you're talking about and he obviously doesn't. You can put him in his place on this point, and that point, and the other point. You can make him feel small. You can teach him a lesson . . . and somewhere down that line you show that you have yourself forgotten the most basic lesson of pastoral care, the one Paul is teaching Timothy here: that the Lord's servant mustn't be a fighter.

How are you going to learn this lesson? Think, for a start, how it was for Jesus. How frustrated he must have been, not only with the wider circle of his hearers but with his friends, his **disciples**. Yet, apart from short sharp rebukes, he normally teased them with another **parable**, coaxed them into looking at things from a different angle, pointed them gently to things they had missed. And ultimately, as the New Testament writers record with awe, he underwent insults, spitting, false accusations, unjust condemnation, torture and a cruel and shameful death, without answering back or giving vent to righteous anger at such unmerited treatment.

It is Jesus himself, his teaching and his example, that has made all the difference in the thinking of Paul and the other early teachers. Paul applies this basic pattern in three ways. First, he advises Timothy simply to steer clear of the sort of disputes that go round and round in circles and get everyone hot and bothered. There is no point even starting that sort of conversation. This isn't weakness – though people who are spoil-ing for a fight will tell you it is if you refuse to join in. It's wisdom.

Second, he urges Timothy to be gentle to *all* people. There are some people it's easy to be gentle with, but there are others who make you want to punch them on the nose as soon as you see them. Being able to teach such people, and particularly to 'bear evil without resentment' (there's one Greek word which says all that, and this is as close as we can get in English), and then to correct opponents with meekness – these are the sure signs that the teacher has been learning from the example, and has been empowered by the **spirit**, of Jesus himself.

Third, he reminds Timothy that after all God himself is the chief pastor. It is God who will do business with people, whether through our ministries or despite them. People may be angry and bitter, opposed to the work of the **gospel** or the detailed teaching which accompanies it. They may have fallen into the trap set for them by the devil (verse 26), not least in themselves becoming 'accusers', ready to find fault and tell people off. Ultimately, it's up to God to soften their hearts and bring them into **repentance** and the right frame of mind. But if that's so, then all our pastoral work is to be seen in terms of our readiness to co-operate with whatever God is doing in their lives. And we cannot help in God's work by using methods – like getting angry in return – that deny the very foundation of the gospel itself.

Learning these lessons is never easy. But they are necessary if we are to purify ourselves from menial tasks and get ready for the really important ones. The irony is, though, that the really important tasks are often the ones that almost nobody else sees. Anybody can put on a good show in public. The real test of a genuine minister of **Christ**, a vessel of gold or silver, pleasing to the master of the house, is whether the metal shines just as brightly when nobody is looking at it.

2 TIMOTHY 3.1–9

Opponents of the Truth

[1]You need to know this: bad times are coming in the last days. [2]People will be in love with themselves, you see, and with money too. They will be boastful, arrogant, abusive, haters of parents, ungrateful, unholy, [3]unfeeling, implacable, accusing, dissolute, savage, haters of the good, [4]traitors, reckless, puffed up, lovers of pleasure rather than lovers of God, [5]holding on to a pattern of godliness but denying its power. Avoid people like that! [6]This group, you see, includes those who worm their way into people's houses and ensnare foolish women who are overwhelmed with their sins and are pulled and pushed by all kinds of desires, [7]always learning but never able to arrive at the truth. [8]Just as Jannes and Jambres stood up against Moses, so people like this oppose the truth. In their minds they are corrupt; in their faith they are of no account. [9]They won't get very far, though, because their foolishness will become obvious to everyone, as it was with those two.

It was a scrappy end to the game, but perhaps it was inevitable. We were winning by what should have been a safe margin; and with a few minutes to go the opposition seemed to realize that their cause was hopeless. Perhaps for that reason, though, they went berserk, as maybe only rugby players can. With nothing more to lose, they threw themselves about the place, fists swinging this way and that, boots flying out to trip or kick. They were furious that we'd won and they wanted to get some revenge in person even if they couldn't on the scoreline. I vividly remember the sigh of relief when the final whistle went and we all trooped off for a bath and to compare bruises.

That sense of the frustration of defeat emerges in various New Testament writings which deal with what seemed at the time to be an increase in human evil. The first letter of John speaks of what it's bound to be like living in the last days. Here Paul says much the same, warning Timothy that the forces of evil, knowing themselves to be defeated in the crucifixion of Jesus, are having a final fling, dragging people into the mud, determined to inflict as much damage on the human race as they can. We who live two thousand years later may find this language of the 'last days' difficult to take, though of course two thousand years, by most people's reckoning, is a tiny fraction of cosmic history. But the early Christians staked their lives on their belief that with the death and **resurrection** of Jesus God's new world had begun, so that the 'last days' had indeed arrived, the interval between the defeat of evil on Calvary and the final defeat that we still await. The point Paul is making, alongside other early writers, is that in this interval, however long or short, we shouldn't expect the world to be steadily improving. We should expect, if anything, an upsurge of evil.

This rules out a misunderstanding people sometimes have of what 'ought to be the case' if it was indeed true that Jesus had won a decisive victory over evil and death through his own death and resurrection. People sometimes object that nothing much seems to have occurred with Jesus because the world is just as bad as it always was. Paul would retort that if anything it's got worse – but, he would add, this doesn't disprove the Christian claim, but rather reinforces it. That's how beaten enemies behave.

The first list he gives of the varied types of evil conduct is quite shocking. We could pause on each type and look in horror at the idea of behaving like that (though recognizing of course that the seeds of all of them are hidden in ourselves as well; there is no cause for complacency or smug self-righteousness). We could investigate each characteristic and ponder the ways in which people get to be like that, the sequence of behaviour choices which they must have made for that to become a settled aspect of their character. But in particular we should

83

notice the effect that behaviour like this – narcissistic, greedy, arrogant, abusive, accusing and so on – has on the people who engage in it, and then, second, the effect it has on all those whose lives are touched by such people.

The first people, those who are actually living that way, are consumed by negative forces and feelings. They are not happy. In fact, they have accepted as a poor substitute for happiness the ability to make others unhappy, so that at least they know they have power over people, even if exercising it makes them miserable themselves (whereupon they need to give themselves a boost by doing more bullying, boasting and so on).

The second people, those whose lives are touched and affected by people who live that way, are (to put it mildly) bruised. They may have developed ways of avoiding the worst pain, but it's a daily battle to stay out of the way, to avoid getting sucked down into a vortex of anger, mutual recrimination, copycat boasting or accusing, and so on.

This type of behaviour, in other words, is not just bad because God happens to forbid it. It isn't as though God drew up a list of rules for human conduct which were arbitrary in the way that the rules of a game might be arbitrary (what's legal in cricket isn't legal in baseball, and vice versa, and this is nothing to do with moral goodness). This sort of thing is bad because it is inherently destructive of human **life**, both the lives of those who perpetrate it and the lives of those who are affected by it. It is an affront to the good creation made by, and loved by, the good creator God.

Worst of all, perhaps, such people often, for whatever reason, take part in religious observances. (Sometimes they have to; alas, the list would include some professional clergy.) But when they do so they are clinging on to the form of godliness, as verse 5 comments, but denying its power. They are going through the motions. But if they stopped to think for two minutes they would realize that in appearing to worship the living God they should be invoking his power and glory to change their lives, to make them reflect his image, not to enable them to go on in the same destructive way as before. This kind of situation arises most painfully when those who have taken part in worship all their lives can't stop even though they don't believe it any more. That is the way to real bitterness. Constantly saying one thing while believing something else is like having continual sharp indigestion, when your bodily system rejects what you're feeding it on.

After the list of awful behaviour in verses 2, 3 and 4, we may be almost amused by Paul saying 'avoid such people'! Well, we would, wouldn't we? But of course for most of the time we don't. Sometimes we can't; we live with them, work with them, sit next to them on the bus. But sometimes we have a choice; and there is no necessary virtue in thinking, 'I'll go and be with so-and-so, even though he's inclined to be nasty from time to time.' There is a time to befriend outsiders; but a young man like Timothy, his character still in formation, is well advised not to associate with those whose behaviour ought not to be copied.

Paul then turns to a much more particular problem. Some of the people he's describing are active in propagating their own views. One of the ways they do this is by preying on the vulnerable. I've seen it happen; I've watched people with particular agendas, and a strong belief in the rightness of their cause, approach people who can't say no to them and persuade them to go to a meeting with them, to listen to their ideas, to join their club. There are many people – the ones Paul seems to have known were women, but many men come into this category too – whose moral or immoral past and whose muddled present makes them easy targets for such predators. They are always hoping that the next new thing they learn will finally sort their lives out; but it never happens, for the good reason that all they really want is the stimulus of novel ideas, not the solid, restful satisfaction of learning the truth and reordering their lives by it.

So who were 'Jannes and Jambres', and when did they oppose Moses? According to ancient Jewish legend, these were the two principal magicians of Egypt referred to in Exodus 7.11 and 7.22. When Moses was performing the God-given signs to convince Pharaoh to let the Israelites go from their slavery, the Egyptian magicians did their best to copy the signs so that Pharaoh wouldn't take Moses seriously. Paul's point is that when the liberating, healing **gospel** is going forwards in power, there will always be people who oppose it by whatever means and tricks they can. His words of comfort ('they won't get very far') are meant to give us hope; in Exodus 7.12, when the magicians turned their staves into snakes as Moses had done, Moses' own serpent ate theirs up. We have to pray and watch for the equivalents in today's church and world. But this hope shouldn't lull us into thinking that there won't be problems to face. We shall need all the good advice of the whole chapter and letter if we are to stay calm and unafraid in the face of the wickedness of the 'last days'.

2 TIMOTHY 3.10–17

Continue in the Scriptures!

[10]So what about you? You have followed my teaching faithfully, and also my way of life, my aims and goals, my faith, longsuffering, love and patience, [11]my persecutions, my sufferings, the things I went

through in Antioch, in Iconium, in Lystra, the persecutions I endured – and the Lord rescued me from all of them. [12]Yes, everyone who wants to live a godly life in Messiah Jesus will be persecuted, [13]while evil people and impostors will go on to even worse things, deceiving others and being themselves deceived. [14]But you, on the other hand, must stand firm in the things you learned and believed. You know who it was you received them from, [15]and how from childhood you have known the holy writings which have the power to make you wise for salvation through faith in Messiah Jesus. [16]All scripture, breathed as it is by God, is useful for teaching, for rebuke, for improvement, for training in righteousness, [17]so that people who belong to God may be complete, fitted out and ready for every good work.

There was once an American professor who went for a year to Oxford as a visiting academic. When he and his wife arrived, they were looking round one of the older parts of the college of which he was to be a member. Amid what appeared to them like the remains of an ancient, crumbling stone building, his wife spotted windows with curtains at them, and people going about their business inside. 'Honey!' she exclaimed, 'These ruins are inhabited!'

It's a true story, and *These Ruins Are Inhabited* became the title of the book she wrote about their experiences that year. For myself, if I visit an old castle or stately home, it gives me a special pleasure to discover that part of it at least is still inhabited by a family who are using it for something like its original purpose. A lived-in building is alive in a way in which a mere tourist attraction, however well laid out, isn't. It breathes.

Many people who open the Bible at random have an experience rather like the woman in Oxford. To begin with, it looks like a jumble of old bits and pieces of writing, a rag-bag of poetry, history, folk tales, ethical instruction and some strange stories about some even stranger people. Reading it can seem, at least to begin with, like wandering through old courtyards where somebody once lived but a long time ago. But then, just when you're tempted to put the whole thing aside as interesting perhaps but not really relevant, you sense movement and **life**. Something is stirring there. There's an energy, as though someone's left a light on or music playing in the old building. Maybe it's inhabited after all. It seems to have a life. A breath, even.

The early Christians believed – and this passage is one of the strong signs of this – that the reason the scriptures were alive was because God had 'breathed' them in the first place, and the warmth and life of that creative breath was still present and powerful. The word 'breathed' in verse 16 is often translated 'inspired', and that word is originally from a Latin word which means pretty much that, 'in-breathed'. But there are three difficulties with the word 'inspired' the way people use it today, and we'd better deal with them at once before seeing what Paul is actually saying here.

First, people often speak of artists and poets, composers and musical performers, and even sports professionals, as being 'inspired'. 'It was an inspired performance', we say, whether at a concert or a football match. What we mean is 'it had something out of the ordinary' or 'it all seemed to come together and work in a new way'. Sometimes we mean that *we* felt 'inspired' by it: it gave us a lift, a boost to the spirits. It was, in that sense, inspir*ing*. The trouble with this meaning of 'inspired' is that it doesn't begin to get near what Paul and other Christian writers mean when they talk about scripture being 'inspired'. They mean what Paul literally says in verse 16: this thing, this book, has living breath in it, and it's the breath of God himself.

Second, when people talk about poets being 'inspired', they sometimes mean that the poet's own mind went into neutral and some other force or spiritual source poured the words in from somewhere else. Some Christians have imagined that when people talk about the Bible being 'inspired', this is the sort of thing they mean: that Jeremiah, Paul and the others functioned as God's typewriter or dictating machine. This can't be right. Those two writers themselves, to look no further, give plenty of evidence that their own personalities, vocations, struggles and sheer individual circumstances affected deeply the way they saw and said things. The inspiration of the Bible didn't flatten out individual styles and angles of vision. If anything, it emphasized them.

Third, many people who insist that the Bible was and is 'inspired' presume that they know in advance what that would mean in terms of the Bible's own content. They presume that it means that the Bible is going to support their particular type of theology. Again and again this has been proved wrong. Precisely because I believe the Bible (rather than anyone's system of theology) is indeed inspired, I am set free from the prison of any human system, free to discover the larger world, the even greater framework of thought, that the Bible itself invites me to share.

Once we set these misunderstandings aside, we should be able to see, and celebrate, the rich unity and diversity of the Bible, and to use it for all it's worth in the many ways which Paul now encourages. Or perhaps we should say, to let it use us: the **spirit** who caused it to be written, who spoke through the different writers in so many ways, is as powerful today as ever, and that power, through the written word, can transform lives. To begin with (verse 15), the spirit speaking through scripture can make us wise – can help us think in new patterns, see things we hadn't seen before, understand ourselves and other people and God and the world ... and ultimately find ourselves rescued, saved, from the downward pull of sin and death, and transformed by God's forgiving grace so that we become part of his new creation. If we let scripture have its way with us, all this is within reach; because, of course, scripture not only unveils the living God we know in Jesus **Christ**, but, through our reading and pondering, it works this knowledge of God deep into our consciousness and even subconsciousness, by story, poetry, symbol, history, theology and exhortation. Scripture not only gives us true information about how our lives can be transformed; it will itself be part of that process.

Paul spells out in verse 16 how this might work. Scripture is useful for teaching; well, of course. For rebuke; that's a bit different. It means, clearly, that as we read scripture it will from time to time inform us in no uncertain terms that something we've been doing is out of line with God's will. Sometimes this will lie plainly on the surface of the text; other times, as we read a passage, we will begin to hear the voice of God gently, or perhaps not so gently, telling us that this story applies to *this* area of our lives, or perhaps *that* one. When that happens – as it may often do for those who read the Bible prayerfully – we do well to pay attention. In addition, though, the rebuke of scripture may be something that Timothy, and others in leadership roles, need to issue to others in the community. This negative possibility is quickly balanced by the positive: reading the Bible will transform you, will 'improve' you, in the sense of somebody making 'improvements' to a house or a city. And it will train you in 'righteousness', which is a combination of goodness and justice, the behaviour that God longs to see in all his children. The aim is (verse 17) not to squash people into a strange, unnatural shape by trying to order their lives according to the Bible, but to help people who belong to God to become complete, richly human beings, reflecting God's image in all its many-sided splendour.

The earlier parts of the passage draw together much that we have already seen in the letter. Like an apprentice, Timothy has had the chance to watch Paul close up and to see what he has gone through and how he has carried on faithfully through it all. He must now learn to stand firm in the things he's learned, even though evil people, both inside the church and outside it, seem to go from bad to worse. It is possible to be deceived, and some of those who are grievously deceived will themselves deceive others, leading to an entire group of people who believe a lie and get angry if people disagree with them – as those who follow the apostolic teaching are bound to do. Life will never be easy for those who live and preach the **gospel**. But with scripture in their heads and their hearts they will be able not only to hold on but to grow in **faith** themselves and to teach others also.

2 TIMOTHY 4.1–5

Judgment Is Coming – So Get On with Your Work

[1]This is my solemn charge to you, in the presence of God and Messiah Jesus, who will judge the living and the dead, and by his appearance and his kingdom: [2]announce the word; keep going whether the time is right or wrong; rebuke, warn and encourage with all patience and explanation. [3]The time is coming, you see, when people won't tolerate healthy teaching. Their ears will start to itch, and they will collect for themselves teachers who will tell them what they want to hear. [4]They will turn away from listening to the truth and will go after myths instead. [5]But as for you, keep your balance in everything! Put up with suffering; do the work of an evangelist; complete the particular task assigned to you.

I was invigilating an exam on a hot summer day. The undergraduates were tired; it was the fourth or fifth exam they had sat already that week, and there were more to come. The sun beat down outside where their friends were waiting to meet them once they had finished. The large clock on the wall moved slowly towards the finishing time.

'You have ten more minutes.' I watched the faces in the room as my voice broke the silence. As usual, there were two quite different responses. Some of the candidates sighed, smiled and sat back. Time was nearly up; not much point trying to do more. Others raised their eyebrows, took a deep breath, and began to write even faster than they had been doing already. Only ten minutes to go! Better get the essay finished. No time to lose.

Examination technique is an odd thing. Some of those who sat back may have known what they were doing. Some of those who wrote even faster may have been disorganized and were simply trying to splash down anything that came into their heads in the vain hope that the examiners might like at least some of it. But I suspected, as I looked around the room, that the first group were simply shrugging their shoulders and giving up, while the second were the ones making the best use of the time.

Paul lived his life with the clock ticking in the background, and he wants Timothy to do the same. Jesus is already enthroned as king of the world, and one day we shall see his royal appearing, the time when the whole world will be held to account. We don't know – we never know – how close to the final day we have come. But we are summoned to live each day, each year, as people ready to give account, ready to face scrutiny, assessment and judgment. For some this might have meant, 'Oh well, it's going to happen soon, so we may as well stop working and give up.' Paul dealt with that attitude in the letters to the Thessalonians. Here he urges Timothy that because judgment is coming it's important to get on with your work.

His description of Timothy's task fits closely with the previous passage, where he's talking about the tasks for which the Bible is useful. Timothy must 'announce the **word**'; as usual, 'the word' here doesn't just mean 'the Bible', though it will include it. 'The word' regularly refers to the Christian **message**, the announcement of Jesus as Lord, which is itself rooted in the scriptures of Israel – the only 'Bible' the earliest Christians had – and focused on telling what happened to Jesus, ramming home the point that, through his **resurrection**, he is now installed as king and Lord.

What's more, Timothy must keep going with this task whether the moment seems propitious or not. As a teacher and preacher, I know that some days just don't seem right. You can't always put your finger on it; but sometimes preaching even a simple sermon, giving a straightforward talk, or counselling someone, becomes really difficult. You have to force the words out. There seems to be no energy anywhere; or, worse, a negative energy working against you. At other times it's different: the words flow effortlessly, things come together, you sense an ease and fluency. There are many different reasons why things should sometimes be difficult: political pressure from outside or inside the community, the wrong or right spiritual atmosphere (to what extent has the church been praying for you in your preparation?), unresolved conflict or evil within the congregation. But how easy it is for preachers then to back off, to give up trying to lead their people into further truth and insight, to trim down the ministry of the word to a few scattered reflections . . . often with the shoulder-shrugging comment that nobody likes sermons these days anyway. And how easy, too, for a preacher who knows that what he or she has to say will be unpopular with some members of the church, or will get them into trouble if the local magistrates hear about it, to trim the content of the teaching down to more general platitudes. Paul, of course, will have none of it. Keep going whether the time is right or wrong!

We know from several things Paul says, both here and in 1 Corinthians, that Timothy was young and perhaps inclined to be shy or anxious. He undoubtedly needed this advice. We probably all know people who inflict their own personality and opinions on everyone they meet, in a brash or even bullying way. Some Christians, alas, are like that, and sometimes justify their behaviour by quoting texts like this. Each of us has to decide which category we fit into and hence which commands are appropriate for us. Perhaps the best rule of thumb is that, if you feel a pressure to tone down or trim down your message, you probably need this advice, whereas if you find yourself eager to get out there and hit people over the head with the Bible, it *may* be that God is calling you to do just that – but it may be that you are using your **faith** as an excuse to indulge your aggressive personality.

The end of verse 2 is very significant. The teacher or preacher is not just to lay down the law. He or she is to make things clear 'with all patience and explanation'. The word for 'explanation' is the general word for 'teaching', but the point in this passage is that it won't do simply to rebuke people, to warn them about the dangers of their present beliefs or behaviour, or to encourage them to continue on a particular course. You need to explain why this is important, to back up what you say with clear teaching, going down to the roots of the subject. This takes patience – something the aggressive or bullying teacher probably hasn't got.

Paul himself now has a warning for Timothy, a warning which explains why he has to go on with his patient teaching. Quite soon, people within the Christian community won't want the kind of teaching which will make and keep them healthy and strong. Like people being instructed by their doctors to follow a particular diet, they will discover that half of their favourite foods aren't on it, and so will look for different doctors who will advise them to eat and drink what they like. In some parts of the Western world there are people who go from church to church trying to find preachers who will tell them what their ears are longing to hear – that they are all right as they are, that they don't need to learn anything more, that they don't have to change their behaviour or obey all those rules . . . and, perhaps in particular, that they needn't believe all that old stuff about Jesus, all the stories you find in the **gospel**s, because there are different stories, different gospels, other ways of looking at Jesus and the world. This is what people often want to hear, and they'll go on looking till they find it. Then (they think) they can rest content. And the church drifts towards the day of Jesus' royal appearing, unaware that accounts have to be presented.

Timothy must be aware of this danger, and must hold his course firmly. Verse 5 is a sober, realistic statement of what Christian ministry is about. You have received a particular calling; get on with it. Keep your balance. It may be difficult or painful at times, but you didn't sign on in order to have an easy life. Go on announcing Jesus as Lord. What is required is not success, as the world regards success, but loyalty and perseverance.

2 TIMOTHY 4.6–8

Waiting for the Crown

> [6]For I am already being poured out as a drink-offering; my departure time has arrived. [7]I have fought the good fight; I have completed the course; I have kept the faith. [8]What do I still have to look for? The crown of righteousness! The Lord, the righteous judge, will give it to me as my reward on that day – and not only to me, but also to all who have loved his appearing.

REWARD: £100,000. The sign stared at me across the road. There was a photograph underneath, and I crossed the street out of curiosity to have a look. It was, of course, a murder suspect. The police were fairly sure they knew who had committed the crime, and were hoping that, if someone was shielding him, the money would be sufficiently attractive to make them come forward and reveal where he was hiding.

'Rewards' like that are one thing. There is no direct connection between the deed (handing someone over to the police) and the reward (lots of money). It's just a payment. But there are different kinds of reward. One schoolchild studies hard to learn Italian because her parents have promised her a new bicycle if she passes the exam. Her neighbour studies equally hard because his family are going to live in Italy and he is looking forward to speaking the language as though he'd lived there all his life. The first reward, like the money the police are offering, has no actual connection with the hard work. The second – the reward of being able to enjoy the new country for all it's worth – is intimately connected to the work. Indeed, it's the direct result of it. It's the most natural sort of 'reward' there is.

Christians sometimes worry about God 'rewarding' people. Does this mean that we are only believing in him, worshipping him and try- ing to obey him because we hope he'll give us (so to speak) a new bicycle, or perhaps £100,000 – or whatever the divine equivalent might be? Well, some people do perhaps start out on the Christian journey thinking like that. Sometimes people have come to a crisis of con- science, perhaps having lived much of their lives without any time for God, and have then tried to twist God's arm to be nice to them after all. That's a poor substitute for genuine worship and love of God – though God remains gracious and merciful, and ready to welcome people however muddled they may be. But it's not what the New Testament has in mind when it speaks of the 'reward' which awaits God's people.

What Paul says in verse 8 corresponds, in fact, to what Jesus said in Matthew 6 (part of the Sermon on the Mount). There, Jesus was talk- ing about the 'reward' which God would give to those who gave away money spontaneously, from the heart: those who fasted and prayed out of genuine penitence and love of God. He was warning against the kind of religion which is all outward show and no inward reality. But he still used the language of 'reward', as Paul does here. We shouldn't be so high-minded as to imagine that the only valid kind of Christian spirituality is that of pure disinterested love of God. Love isn't like that, anyway. When you love someone, part of the 'reward' is the joy of being able to do things with and for them, and of being loved by them in turn.

The worry that many people have is related more particularly to the doctrine of '**justification** by **faith**'. Paul insists, especially in Romans and Galatians, that our 'good works' will not justify us. But it's clear in those passages that he's talking about our *present* standing before God. Whenever he talks about the future, final judgment, on the great coming 'day of the Lord', he always speaks of it as related not just to our faith, but to the total substance of our lives. (See, for instance, Romans 2.1–16 or 2 Corinthians 5.6–10.) Paul would of course say that this total **life** was itself the result, not of his own unaided efforts, but of the hard work he had accomplished through the **holy spirit** at work within him. That's more or less exactly what he says in passages like 1 Corinthians 15.10 and Colossians 1.19. As with the logic of love, so with the logic of working for God in the power of the spirit: God retains the initiative, and remains the ultimate source of energy, but the Christian is called and required to work hard *with* that energy. And when he or she does so, there will be an appropriate reward – not an arbitrary gift like the money or the bicycle, but a glory and honour within God's new world which corresponds to the kind of work that has been done.

Paul frames this hope for an appropriate reward within four overlapping pictures – mixing up his metaphors in his usual style. He begins with the (to him) well-known picture of an animal being sacrificed, with worshippers pouring drink-offerings on top of it. As in Philippians 2.17, he's referring to his own probably imminent death as being like that sort of drink-offering; presumably the **sacrifice** on which it's to be poured is, as in that passage, the worship and faith of the churches he has founded. But he quickly changes the picture, and we find ourselves in the athletics stadium – perhaps even the amphitheatre, for a gladiatorial contest. Paul has fought the fight, not an ordinary fight but the 'good' or 'noble' fight. He has run the course and stayed on track. That's why he then talks about the 'crown', the badge which would be awarded to the winner, like an Olympic medal today.

But as soon as he mentions the crown, and the fact that the Lord himself will give it to him, he changes the picture again, and we find ourselves in the lawcourt. The Lord is the one just and righteous judge, the one who can be relied upon to come up with exactly the right verdict. Paul trusts him totally and knows that he will vindicate him at his tribunal. This, we may guess, is in contrast to the other judges he has already faced and will shortly face once more (see verse 16). And among these judges Paul may very well number, as their chief, the emperor himself.

That would explain why, once more, Paul talks about Jesus' 'royal appearing'. The fourth of the pictures is the now familiar one of citizens waiting to greet the emperor. Some of them are delighted; they are keen supporters of the emperor, and love the very thought that soon he will appear before them. Others resent his rule, and would rather they were free of it. So it will be with the 'appearing' of Jesus himself; and Paul knows that not only he, but all who 'love his appearing' will be rewarded on the final day when it happens. Being poured out like a drink-offering while winning a race which results in being vindicated in the lawcourt and so being ready for the true emperor to arrive . . . who but Paul could write a paragraph like that? Are we ready to think as creatively as he was about the tasks and the goal we face today?

2 TIMOTHY 4.9–22

Come to Me Soon

⁹Make every effort to come to me soon. ¹⁰Demas, you see, has left me and gone to Thessalonica; he's in love with this present world! Crescens has gone to Galatia, and Titus to Dalmatia. ¹¹Luke is the only one with me. Get Mark and bring him with you; he's very helpful in looking after me. ¹²I sent Tychicus to Ephesus. ¹³I left a cloak at Carpus' house in Troas; please bring it with you when you come – and also the scrolls, and especially the books.

¹⁴Alexander the coppersmith did me a lot of damage. The Lord will pay him back according to what he's done! ¹⁵Watch out for him yourself. He stood out strongly against our message.

¹⁶The first time my case came to court nobody showed up to support me; they all left me alone. May it not be reckoned against them! ¹⁷But the Lord stood there beside me and gave me strength to enable me to complete my work as his royal herald, and to make sure that all the Gentiles heard the proclamation; and I was snatched clear of the lion's mouth. ¹⁸The Lord will snatch me clear from every wicked deed and will save me for his heavenly kingdom. Glory to him for the ages of ages, Amen!

¹⁹Greet Prisca and Aquila, and the household of Onesiphorus. ²⁰Erastus stayed in Corinth. I left Trophimus behind in Miletus, where he was sick.

²¹Do your best to come before winter.

Eubulus sends his greetings; so do Pudens, Linus, Claudia, and all the family.

²²The Lord be with your spirit. Grace be with you all.

One of the accidental spin-offs from early Christianity was the invention of the book.

There may have been some primitive books before, but these were different. Most writing in the ancient world was either on clay tablets or on parchment scrolls, rolled up on a stick at either end. They were cumbersome and difficult to use. You couldn't keep two passages open at once. Nor could you get very much material on to a single scroll. At the most, a scroll might contain a book about as long as one of the **gospel**s.

But the early Christians wanted to be able to have several of these books quite literally bound up together. If you stitch or glue sheets of paper or papyrus together, you can hold a lot more material in your hand. You can have, for example, all four gospels in one volume. And you can study them far more easily than having to work through a scroll. You can keep your place at several different points, and go to and fro to compare them. It looks as though the early Christians, by collecting the writings which formed the foundation charter of their movement, in particular the writings about Jesus, were innovators in the art of book-binding. Before long the 'codex', as it was called, became their preferred format, rather than the scroll.

What we see in verse 13 is a sign of this process in its very early stage. Paul asks Timothy to come to him as soon as he can; winter is approaching, and he's afraid he's going to be cold without his own old cloak. He had left it in Troas (Troy, in the north-west corner of modern Turkey), and wants Timothy to bring it with him when he comes to him. But at the same time there are more precious things: the scrolls and the books. Some translators have made the first word into 'books' and the second into 'parchments', as though the former were like our books and the latter were, perhaps, Paul's own notebooks; but it's more likely that by the first word Paul was referring to a set of scrolls, each containing a smallish amount of material, and that the second does indeed refer to what we call books, i.e. sheets of paper stuck or stitched together next to one another, forming a flat volume.

What these scrolls and books contained is of course a matter of guesswork. But if they were important enough for Paul to ask, quite urgently, that Timothy should bring them, we may guess with some plausibility that they were parts of what we now call the New Testament. They contained, maybe, at least one of the gospels, and perhaps other

95

early documents which were then incorporated into the other gospels as we know them today. This little reference, in fact, is both fascinating and frustrating. It tells us enough to excite our curiosity, but not enough to satisfy it. Paul was clearly concerned to keep up his own reading and study, not least to be able to ponder and mull over the stories about, and teachings of, Jesus himself. But if only he could have told Timothy in a little more detail what was in those scrolls and books!

The same is true about all the personal details in this closing passage. We are fascinated by this glimpse of Paul in prison, with some of his followers going off, some being sent with messages for other churches or jobs to do, others possibly coming to visit. We would love to know more about where exactly Paul was, and how all the travelling and visiting fitted together. We're like someone driving past a house at night; we get a glimpse through the open window of a lighted room with people coming and going, and they look interesting, but before we can find out any more about them we are too far down the road, and the glimpse remains a memory.

That doesn't mean there's nothing to learn from this passage except how fascinating and frustrating historical documents can be! The centre of this rather scattered closing sequence shows Paul reflecting one more time on his task as the royal herald of King Jesus, this time on the opportunity he had, when on trial for his life, to speak up for the **message** about his master. All the other Christians in town (we presume it's Rome, because of 1.17; but some people have thought it might be while Paul was in prison in Caesarea, as in Acts 23—26) had been too frightened to show up in court to support Paul. This must have been a cruel blow. But Paul doesn't hold it against them, and doesn't want God to either. Instead of human support, Paul was powerfully aware that the Lord himself had been with him, giving him strength. As he stood there in court, he was able to speak of Jesus as the **Messiah**, the world's true Lord, and realized that he was being given a chance, perhaps a final one, to complete his work as Jesus' royal herald, this time with senior and influential non-Jews listening.

When he says that he was rescued from the lion's mouth, he probably doesn't mean it literally. He was a Roman citizen, and made good use of the fact; Roman citizens didn't get sent to the arena to be eaten by wild beasts, certainly not in this period. If Paul was to be executed, it would be by the sword. However, as he looks at the Roman empire he sees it, as Daniel 7 would have done, as a dangerous monster, a wild animal, ready to devour anyone who speaks up for 'another king'. What neither the empire nor any of its monsters (actual or metaphorical) can do, however, is to prevent the Lord rescuing Paul from their evil intentions and giving him the glorious status of a member of the coming

kingdom. At present this kingdom is a **heaven**ly reality; one day it will be earthly as well.

Meanwhile, there are people to know about and pray about. I can't help feeling sorry for Demas, who shows up with Paul in Colossians 4.14 and Philemon 24; this passage puts him in a bad light, and leaves an unfortunate taste in the mouth. We may hope that, whatever his 'being in love with this present world' meant in practice, his knowledge of Paul, and still more his knowledge of Jesus **Christ**, was strong enough to bring him back to full allegiance to the gospel. This has happened, clearly, with Mark, who abandoned Paul on his first missionary journey (Acts 13.13, where he is confusingly called by his other name, 'John'), but whom Paul now regards as a useful and helpful companion. As for Alexander the coppersmith, he may be the same man who was trying to make trouble for Paul in the riot at Ephesus (Acts 19.33). He probably isn't the one whom Paul refers to in 1 Timothy 1.20. ('Alexander' was a very common name throughout the ancient Mediterranean world, ever since Alexander the Great three centuries before.)

The picture we get, as we take leave of this intimate and personal letter, is of a man facing serious trouble and likely death, beset with problems and anxieties, but who nevertheless remains determined to bring every single aspect of his **life** into the orbit of the gospel itself, the royal proclamation of Jesus as Lord. He lives in the present world, Caesar's world, as already a cheerful citizen of the world to come, Jesus' world. He longs to see Timothy working hard and effectively for Jesus as he himself has done. And, as we listen in to his end of the conversation, we are left in no doubt as to what kind of advice he would give us today.

TITUS

TITUS 1.1−4

God's Revealed Plan

> [1]From Paul, a slave of God and an apostle of Jesus the Messiah, in accordance with the faith of God's chosen people, and the knowledge of the truth that goes with godliness, [2]in the hope of the life of the coming age. God, who never lies, promised this before the ages began, [3]and has now, at the right time, unveiled his word through the proclamation entrusted to me, according to the command of our divine saviour.
>
> [4]To Titus, my true child, according to the faith which we share.
> Grace and peace from God the father and Messiah Jesus our saviour.

'What do you want to be when you grow up?'

It's the standard question children face from well-meaning adults. Often the answers are surprising. A ballet dancer. A gardener. This girl wants to run a bookshop. This boy wants to play the oboe. Sometimes the dreams are fantasies, and melt away in the light of grown-up life. Sometimes they are the first shoots of a deep sense of identity and vocation that come into full blossom and fruit later on. Children are aware, often with a sense of frustration, that there are basically two 'ages', childhood and adulthood, and that they have to wait before they can attempt to turn their dreams into reality – though one sign that the dream will become reality is the determination to begin in the present to study and train to make it happen.

Deep within the mind and imagination of most first-century Jews lay the belief that world history itself is divided into two 'ages': the **present age** and the **age to come**. They didn't usually see this in terms of childhood and adulthood – the break would be more convulsive than that – but there are several parallels between the way they thought about history and the way children see the future. *Now* we are frustrated, hemmed in by the world that isn't yet all that it will be. *Then* everything will be different; we shall be able to start our real life and show what we're made for. *Now* we, God's people, are being oppressed by wicked nations that don't know the true God, but worship idols and follow tyrannical leaders. *Then* we shall be free, and will share God's own rule of his glorious new world.

Paul believed firmly in this two-age scheme, and it remained central to all his thinking and living as a Christian. He does actually use the child/adult picture as an illustration for it, in 1 Corinthians 13.11. One of the principal differences between him and those of his fellow Jews who didn't accept Jesus as **Messiah** then becomes clear: he believed that the future had come forwards into the present, the *then* into the *now*, in the person of Jesus and the proclamation which he, Paul, was called upon to make. When he announced that God had raised Jesus from the dead, and installed him as king, Lord and saviour, he was introducing God's new age into the middle of the existing one.

Thus, even in the introduction to a short letter, Paul locates his work and his writing within the larger framework of God's overall plan – like someone sketching a map of the entire country in order to pinpoint a single small village.

We find the sketch in verses 2 and 3. God promised that there would be a 'coming age', with a whole new quality of '**life**'. This promise has turned into a public announcement through Paul's work of proclaiming Jesus.

God doesn't lie. He can be trusted absolutely. Paul's **gospel** is founded on the rock-solid basis of the reliability, the trustworthiness, the faithfulness of the one true God. This was extraordinary news to the average first-century pagan, who was used to there being many gods, none of whom could be relied upon. The only thing you really knew about the gods was that there were a lot of them, and that at any moment this god, or perhaps that goddess, might either take a fancy to you and do something really nice, or take a dislike to you (perhaps you'd forgotten to offer a **sacrifice** at the right time, or the appropriate place) and punish you. The gods were unpredictable, potentially dangerous, or even malevolent. Part of the '**good news**' of the early Christian gospel was that the One True God, the God of Israel, was now making himself known in and to all the world as the utterly reliable God, the one you could trust.

This, in fact, is the force of the opening verse. Paul introduces himself as a slave of this God, and an **apostle** – an emissary, an accredited herald – of Jesus as the true king. The status he has in relation to God and Jesus comes directly from 'the **faith** of God's chosen people' and 'the knowledge of the truth that goes with godliness'. Paul claims that in Jesus as Messiah the age-old faith of Israel has now been vindicated, that the gospel message is rooted in God's faithfulness to his promises and shaped by the ancient Israelite beliefs. This leads to a knowledge of the truth: not just guesswork, not just humans groping in the dark to try to discover something about God, but a revealed truth you can stake your life on. It's a knowledge which goes hand in hand with the kind of devotion Paul calls 'godliness' or 'piety', by which he means not simply a general religious attitude to life (many pagans had that, and it didn't do them much good) but a willingness to allow one's whole life, from prayer to public action, to be shaped by the calling and will of God.

Paul and Titus share this faith, and it appears from Paul's calling him his 'child' that Titus learned it from Paul himself. We don't know very much about Titus. We know he was born a Greek, a **Gentile**, and that this caused trouble with the strict Jewish Christians when he accompanied Paul to Jerusalem (Galatians 2.1–3). We know that he accompanied Paul on his final journey to Corinth, because the second letter to Corinth speaks of him going on ahead and then returning to bring Paul news from the Corinthians (2 Corinthians 2.13, 7.6–14 and elsewhere). We know that at some later stage, while in prison, Paul sent him to Dalmatia (2 Timothy 4.10). But apart from that we are left in the dark. Curiously, he is never mentioned in Acts. Just as Paul (who could have said a lot about his family background and so on) wanted to be known as 'a slave of God and an apostle of Jesus', so we simply know Titus as a child of Paul in the faith, and a loyal one at that.

As the natural blessing from father to son, and indeed from God's 'coming age' to the 'present age', Paul opens the letter by wishing Titus the two central blessings of the gospel: 'grace and peace'. Grace speaks of God as the source of all the blessings we enjoy; peace summarizes those blessings, indicating the primary reconciliation between God and humans and the secondary reconciliations between one person or community and another. In the church where I work we sometimes use this as the opening greeting in a service: 'Grace to you and peace from God the father and the Lord Jesus **Christ**'. I hope these words never become an empty formula. Certainly for Paul they were always full of meaning, alive with hope and promise.

And also with cheerful subversion. As we saw in 1 and 2 Timothy, in these Pastoral Letters, Paul regularly refers to Jesus with a title the Roman world used for Caesar: 'saviour'. Caesar claimed to have rescued, or 'saved', the world from chaos, war and anarchy. The early Christians claimed that Jesus had saved it from the ultimate chaos of sin and death. The new world had broken into the old, summoning it to grow up and discover what it was meant to be.

TITUS 1.5–9

Appointing Elders

> [5]This is why I left you in Crete: you are to set straight all the remaining matters, and appoint elders for every town, as I charged you to do. [6]Elders must be blameless, the husband of only one wife. Their children must be believers, and must not be open to the accusation of loose living, or being rebellious. [7]This is because an overseer, as one of God's household managers, must be blameless. He must not be

stubborn, or hotheaded, or a heavy drinker, or a bully, or eager for shameful gain. [8]He must be hospitable, a lover of goodness, sensible, just, holy and self-controlled. [9]He must hold firmly to the reliable word which goes with the teaching, so that he may have the power both to exhort people with healthy instruction and to give a proper rebuttal to those who oppose it.

The worst moment was when we realized the pilot had no idea what to do next.

We were travelling in a light aircraft, going north from Pretoria in South Africa into Zimbabwe, or Rhodesia as it was then called. There were five of us in the plane: the pilot, our two hosts, my wife and myself. There had been some mechanical problems earlier on, but they had been fixed – or so we thought – before we left Pretoria. Now we were flying north. We crossed the Limpopo, and found ourselves over open bushland, on and on for miles. But the plane's electrical systems had started to fail. We lost radio contact. The automatic direction finder stopped working. Even the petrol gauge packed up. All that was working was the engine itself. Without any landmarks anywhere, we were lost. Only the sun told us roughly which direction we were going in, not how far we'd come. With strong side winds, we couldn't tell whether we were drifting east or overcorrecting; either way we might miss our destination (Harare, then called Salisbury) by a long way.

We might not have realized how serious the situation was if the pilot had not turned round to talk to us. He was biting his nails, a bad sign. He explained the position, or rather the lack of it. He had no idea where we were, and in any case there weren't any airports in the region where we could come down and get the plane fixed, or even stay the night. He handed the map back to us with an air of desperation. 'Well,' he said, 'you see if you can figure out where we are!' We couldn't.

We reached Salisbury more by providence than skill (after several hours, we crossed a road, and flew down to read the road signs; fortunately it was still daylight, but only just). But I learned an important lesson that day. When the pilot can't figure out what's going on, the whole plane is in trouble.

That is the principle behind Paul's very detailed instructions about the character of elders, those leaders in the church who are to preside and look after the community. (He sometimes calls them 'elders', as in verse 6, and sometimes 'overseers', as in verse 7. The word for 'overseer' is the word from which we get the word 'bishop'. This passage makes it look as though the two offices at least overlapped at this stage, and may have been identical.) We might have thought that, with only a small handful of Christians in every place, Paul or Titus would have had to rest content with finding what leaders they could, appointing anyone with a bit of natural authority or common sense. But no. Paul would rather have no leader at all than one whose character didn't match the **message**. If you can't rely on church leaders to model Christian character, how can you expect anyone else in the church to bring their lives into the pattern of **Christ**? If they don't know how to read the map, how to tell where they are in the uncharted bushland of cultural and social pressure, in the winds and storms of temptation, greed, fear and selfish desire, how on earth can the passengers be expected to help?

Titus is now faced with the apparently unenviable task of finding, in every town, people who will be able to lead and guide the church without falling prey to any of these dangers. I say 'apparently' unenviable because in fact one of the great joys of Christian leadership is discovering the hundreds of ways in which God has been at work in the hearts and lives of all kinds of people, drawing them not only to **faith** but to an attractive devotion and holiness of life, and equipping them for different kinds of ministries and service. There are a great many people, in fact, who have quietly got on and reformed their lives under the leading of the **spirit** and in obedience to the word of the **gospel**. They haven't thought they were doing anything special, just trying to live in glad and grateful response to the message which has brought them new **life** and hope. There are times in church work when one is tempted to despair of finding leaders to take the work forwards; but again and again one discovers that the holy spirit is not so short of resources as we might have thought. Titus may well find that there are sufficient candidates.

It is still a daunting prospect. Many of the qualifications have to do with the need for leaders, being in the public eye, to be above the sneering reproach or criticism of the outside world. Not only must one's family life be above reproach – which, as all clergy with families know, is difficult enough. One's own character must ring true at point after point. It's no good being a fine preacher, a wise pastor and a competent administrator if, every few days, you fly off the handle and yell at people. It's no good being a great church organizer and leader if the way you accomplish your goals is by bullying. And so on. The elder, or bishop, must be someone who can face every situation that comes and respond with Christlike wisdom and self-control.

Nor is this simply reactive (how people behave when confronted with different challenges). It's about taking initiatives as well. The leader must be hospitable. He or she must take the lead in teaching, and in doing so must show a firm grasp, both in outline and detail, of the gospel of Jesus, rooted in the word of scripture. When people oppose healthy teaching, as, alas, some will always do, there is a temptation to avoid confrontation, to back off and hope they will go away. They won't. The leader – this is a particular function of elders and bishops, and one which doesn't normally gain them popularity – must know how to rebut false teaching.

The fashionable stance in today's Western world is against strong, clear teaching. People are suspicious of those who claim that we can be certain about some things. Many today prefer the flexible world where you can't be sure about anything and each person has to find the way for themselves. That has never been the Christian position, and it shouldn't be now. Of course there are lots of things we can't be sure about. Of course there is new knowledge waiting to be discovered. Of course some of the things people thought they knew three hundred years ago must now be challenged, or expressed afresh. Nobody should doubt that. But equally there are many things upon which the church, and especially its leaders, must be clear and emphatic. Some of those who insist upon their certainties have done so in a bullying, stubborn fashion; that is, of course, ruled out by verse 7. But just because there is such a thing as arrogance, that doesn't mean there isn't such a thing as firm and well-grounded faith, expressed in loving clarity. May God give the church leaders who can teach like that.

TITUS 1.10–16

The Problems in Crete

[10]There are many, you see, who refuse to come into line – people who speak foolishness and deceive others. This is true in particular of the circumcision party. [11]It's important that they should be silenced, because they are overturning whole households by teaching things that shouldn't be taught – and trying to make a shameful living out of it! [12]One of their own, a native prophet, said, 'Cretans are always liars, evil animals, idle guzzlers.' [13]This testimony is true! That's why you must rebuke them sternly, so that they may become healthy in the faith, [14]paying no attention to Jewish myths and the commandments of people who reject the truth. [15]Everything is pure to people who are pure. But if people are defiled or faithless, nothing is pure for them; even their mind and conscience are defiled. [16]They declare that they know God, but they deny him by what they do. They are detestable and disobedient, and useless for any good work.

There is a famous puzzle which young philosophers love. Imagine a postcard, blank on both sides except for a single sentence on each. You pick it up and read it.

The side you're looking at says, 'The statement on the other side of this card is true.'

Intrigued, you turn it over.

On the back it says, 'The statement on the other side of this card is false.'

Slowly, you turn it back again and start to figure it out. If you are determined, or patient, or perhaps just stubborn, you may still be standing there many hours later.

Another version of the same puzzle is found in this passage, and has become known as the 'Cretan liar paradox'. Paul certainly regarded it as funny. (This should alert us to the fact that he is probably writing 'tongue in cheek' for at least some of the time in this passage. This is part of the difficulty of reading ancient texts, and even some modern ones; something which the author intended to be taken with a twinkle in the eye can come across on the page as though it's heavy-handed and dismissive.) He quotes someone from Crete saying, 'Everybody in Crete always tells lies' – and then he says that *this* testimony is true! We turn the postcard over and find . . . that Paul is laughing, not unkindly, but finding ways of warning Titus that he's going to have to be robust and be prepared to work with the people of Crete. Paul has left him there with a job to do (1.5), in order to instruct them and change their famous, or perhaps we should say notorious, national characteristic.

But the main thing Paul is anxious about in this paragraph is that many people in Crete seem to have taken up with some kind of Judaism. His reference in verse 10 to 'the **circumcision** party' reminds us of Galatians 2.10, where he uses the same phrase to refer to a group of Jewish Christians who were insisting that **Gentile** converts should be circumcised so that they could be seen to be obeying the **law** of Moses. Paul dealt with that question fully in Galatians, but other parts of the church still needed to learn the lesson. Here he doesn't go into the theological arguments as to why circumcision is not to be required, but instead warns against the general tone of the Jewish commands that people would try to foist onto new converts.

To begin with, he warns that such people – he calls them 'agitators' in Galatians – can have a very disruptive effect. Once you introduce the idea that there is an 'inner circle' of Christians who, by becoming Jews as well, have entered a new, special area from which mere uncircumcised believers in Jesus are excluded, you can imagine the effect it's likely to have on families and households who have accepted the **faith**. Instead of unity and a common mind, there will be division, suspicion and rivalry. Again, this had happened in Galatia and Paul didn't want to see it happening in Crete or anywhere else. He implies, too, that the people who were trying to teach the Jewish law to newly converted Christians were hoping to make money out of it. Plenty of wandering teachers in the ancient world did that – offering a new, special initiation, accompanied by teaching about mysteries, rituals and the like, and demanding payment for their services.

Then, after repeating the joke about Cretan liars, Paul urges Titus to help the people in his care to understand what truth, and the Truth, are all about. The false teachers who may dog his footsteps will probably try to teach the converts stories about the Jewish heroes of old, developing the biblical narratives of the patriarchs and prophets in various ways. We have whole books from this period of Judaism which attempted to draw out lessons for their own time by expanding the stories in the Bible into apocalyptic visions, dramatic incidents, lengthy dialogues and so on. Again and again these are designed to persuade people that they should keep the Jewish law – not so much the Ten Commandments (which Paul himself reinforces in various places) but the aspects of Jewish law which were, effectively, a barrier between Jews and Gentiles. Paul dismisses all that kind of thing. It is, he says in verse 14, a collection of merely human commands which goes against the truth (presumably he means the truth of the **gospel**, as in Galatians 2.5 and 2.14).

In particular, such teachers emphasized that there were some things, particularly some foods, which were ritually impure and should be avoided completely. The way to know the true God, they would teach, was to abstain from everything impure and hold fast to the law. Paul rejects this severely, echoing as he does so the teaching of Jesus himself in passages like Mark 7. True purity isn't a matter of touching this and not touching that. True purity (verse 15) is a matter of the person concerned having their mind renewed and conscience educated, not a matter of one kind of meat being pure and another being impure. 'To the pure all things are pure'; this saying has passed into common speech as a kind of proverb. It doesn't mean, of course, that one can do whatever one wants; there are plenty of things which genuinely pure people won't want to do at any price (oppression, fraud, violence, sexual immorality and so on). But the trouble is that if people are not pure in themselves then everything they touch will become defiled, however pure it is in itself. They can keep what regulations they like and it will make no difference.

Their mind and conscience will remain in a state of impurity – in other words, of being excluded from the only inner circle that matters, namely, the knowledge of God. Those who keep all the purity laws may well claim that they are thereby 'knowing God', but in fact they may be denying the true God with every breath they take.

Titus is not to compromise with such people. He isn't to soften Paul's hard line. Teaching like that is to be rejected from top to bottom, and people who hold it and propagate it won't be any use in building up the community. Harsh words for hard realities. Applying all this will take courage. Titus has Paul's own example if he wants reminding of what that looks like in practice.

TITUS 2.1–10

Commands to Households

[1]So what must you do? Just this: you must instruct people how to conduct themselves in accordance with healthy teaching.

[2]The older men are to be sober, dignified, sensible, and healthy in faith, love and patience. [3]In the same way, older women are to be reverent in their behaviour, not slanderers or enslaved to heavy drinking, able to teach what is good. [4]That way, they can give sensible instructions to the younger women on how to love their husbands and their children, [5]and how to be sensible, holy, good at looking after the household, and submissive to their own husbands, so that people won't have bad things to say about the word of God. [6]You must urge the younger men, in the same way, to be sensible [7]in all things.

Make sure you present yourself as a pattern of good works. Your teaching must be consistent and serious, [8]in healthy speech that is beyond reproach. That way, our opponents will be ashamed, since they won't have anything bad to say about us.

[9]Slaves must be submissive in everything to their masters. They must do what is wanted and not answer back [10]or help themselves to their masters' property. They are to show good faith in everything, so that in every way they may be a good advertisement for the teaching of God our saviour.

I was at a meeting yesterday of the governors of a local school. The head teacher was presenting his annual report. With pardonable pride he described how the school choir had gone on a tour around three Canadian cities, singing in cathedrals, churches and concert halls. He quoted from some of the letters he had received after they'd got back. One described how, in addition to inspiring and immaculate singing, the children in the choir had behaved throughout the entire tour with grace, poise and charm. They were, said the writer (himself a leading teacher and musician), perfect ambassadors for the country and the school.

People are watching all the time. When it's a school choir, they almost expect that when young performers are not on stage they will relax and maybe kick over the traces a little. That hadn't happened in this case, and people remarked on it. The watching world takes note. The same happens, for instance, with a seminary rugby team – a formidable proposition. Will there be bad language in the scrum? Will there be cheating when the referee's back is turned? If there is, people will look at each other and smile knowingly. Maybe these priests-in-training aren't so holy after all.

But what if there's a town in the ancient Mediterranean world which has never seen Christians before? This is a new community, organizing itself in a new way, refusing to join in with normal public events like the **sacrifices** which celebrate the various gods and goddesses, including the special local ones. Its members no longer frequent the drunken orgies they once did. They are even rumoured to refuse to take the oath of allegiance to the emperor . . . people will be watching. What sort of folk are these Christians? Are they really a secret society holding wild parties when nobody is watching? Are they going to be a social nuisance? Might they be a political embarrassment?

Well, they might turn out to be awkward in various ways. Certainly their refusal to join in the regular sacrifices and pagan ceremonies wouldn't win them any friends. And their attitude to Caesar, though careful and not at this stage confrontative, could have got them into trouble. But Paul, like other early Christian teachers, is anxious that if the Christians are going to get into trouble it will be because of things they definitely stand for, not because of incidental things which people on the street will mock or sneer at but which Christians should in any case avoid.

High on the list, in this letter and several others, comes the ordered integrity of family life. Today, of course, people sneer at family life. Many in fashionable Western society regard it as dispensable, a hangover from an older day when people were cowed and submissive, when a bullying father figure ruled the household with a rod of iron. We're free, people say; we don't have to live like that any more. To insist on household rules for women, children and slaves is to turn the clock back. If someone really ran their household the way Paul seems to be urging in this passage, some neighbours might report them to the police.

As I've pointed out in other passages, the most striking item in this list of instructions – the commands to slaves in verses 9 and 10 – is to be seen, of course, in the setting of ordinary daily life in the first century. Slavery was a fact of life and there was no point pretending it wasn't. You could no more abolish slavery overnight in the first century than you could invent space travel. The fact that you might hope it would happen one day, and wished it would, wouldn't justify giving slaves the impression that now they were Christians they could disobey their masters – any more than a futuristic fantasy about space travel would have justified Paul in selling tickets to Mars. That isn't an exact parallel, of course, but it makes the point that the early Christians worked within what was possible at the time, while constantly lodging protests against abuses within the system and, where they could, against the system itself (the letter to Philemon is the best example).

The vital thing was that slaves, having become Christians, shouldn't regard themselves as above the law. Some might think, 'Because my master isn't a Christian, and I am, this gives me a right to tell him what's what – after all, I'm a servant of the King of the World and he isn't!' What message would that send to the watching world of Crete or anywhere else? It would indicate that this new cult was simply making trouble and ought to be stamped out. No: Christian slaves, like Christians in every walk of life, must be good advertisements, good ambassadors, for 'the teaching of God our saviour'.

The same is true, less controversially though still surprisingly to some today, within the extended families where many people lived then, as in some parts of the Mediterranean world they still do. To this day in parts of Greece and Turkey there are homes with two or three generations, maybe even more, living under one roof, often working together on the same farm or family business. The danger in that kind of setting is that life degenerates into a round of gossip and backchat, and from that into jealousy and spite, all lubricated by alcohol, with the senior members of the family either abdicating responsibility or bullying the others into temporary sullen silence. All that must stop. The senior men – notice that they receive their instructions first, because if they want to hold respect, as they would, they must first learn to set an example for everyone else – the men must not get drunk, they must not be grumpy or churlish. Likewise the older women (this might mean women from as young as thirty) must not allow themselves to turn to drink or gossip; they are to set a good example of sensible behaviour and show the next generation that things will work much better in family life if everyone gets on with their tasks and fits into the structure than if everyone grumbles and tries to buck the system.

Once more, this kind of advice sounds, I know, awfully boring and old-fashioned. Perhaps half the novels, plays and films that appear today are about people kicking over the traces, 'discovering their real identity', breaking out of the social and cultural prisons other people had put them in, and so on. No doubt there are oppressive structures; no doubt there are plenty of people who need to escape from them. But there is a spurious form of freedom which has more in common with an atomic particle whizzing randomly all over the place than with the genuine liberty which sets you free to be yourself in the appropriate framework.

True freedom is never mere anarchy. Being a rebel is fine, sometimes even necessary; but it can't be the only thing you believe in and do, or you end up isolated, lonely and aimless. Even revolutionaries, when they're successful, discover that they then have to reinvent social structures in order to get on with the business of life. Far more important, especially if you're part of a small and struggling Christian community, is to live with integrity in the framework you've got, and make your witness to the **gospel** tell by refusing to give outsiders any chance to mock or criticize your home and family life.

TITUS 2.11–15

Grace, Hope and Holiness

[11]God's saving grace, you see, appeared for all people. [12]It teaches us that we should turn our backs on ungodliness and the passions of the world, and should live sober, just and devout lives in the present age, [13]while we wait eagerly for the blessed hope and royal appearing of the glory of our great God and saviour, Jesus the Messiah. [14]He gave himself for us so that he could ransom us from all lawless actions and purify for himself a people as his very own who would be eager for good works.

[15]This is what you must say. Exhort people and rebuke them. Use full authority. Don't let anyone look down on you.

Soon after the Russian revolution, a group of journalists and social commentators paid a visit to the newly formed Soviet Union to see how the revolutionaries were getting on in establishing a new type of society. They were shown the model communities in which property had been pooled ('collectivized'). Production was booming and everyone seemed happy in the new, classless society.

Among the journalists was an American called Lincoln Steffens. He wrote to a friend about it. 'I have seen the future,' he said, 'and it works.' Actually, Steffens had written the line before the trip even began, but it was obviously too good not to use; he had *imagined* the future, and then of course was eager to see that his prediction was true. He and the others were so impressed that they reckoned this was the way that the whole world should go, and, what's more, would go in time. They convinced many in Europe and America, not least those who were appalled by the devastating First World War and at the casual way tyrannical rulers had (so it seemed) sent millions to their deaths. Having glimpsed the future of a world, as they thought, run according to the dictates of communism, they believed that they should now work to make it a reality.

Nearly a century later, of course, the claim looks hollow. Between 1919 and 1989 (when the Berlin Wall fell, signalling the collapse of Eastern European communism) the totalitarian states of the East proved themselves just as capable of creating a future that did *not* work as any of the other systems that had been tried from time to time. The pendulum swung in the other direction. Thirty years after Steffens, the sharp-eyed George Orwell gave to one of his characters the following line: 'If you want a picture of the future, imagine a boot stamping on a human face – for ever.' Orwell's bleak vision of the future had a different moral: if this is how things are going to be, you should either lie very low indeed or take care that you're on the winning side.

Paul's appeal about how people should live is built firmly on his belief that the future has already appeared in the present, and that we are all now summoned to act in accordance with it. This future-in-the-present has appeared, though, not in the form of a dramatic new social experiment, nor in the shape of yet another oppressive regime stamping on everyone in its path, but in the form of the death and **resurrection** of Jesus. Paul doesn't mention this explicitly, but it's obviously what he has in mind in verse 11 when he talks about 'God's saving grace' appearing for all people. The events of Jesus' **life**, death and resurrection were, for him, the moment when, and the means by which, the generous and powerful love of God (that's what he means by 'grace') were unveiled for the benefit, not of one group of people only, but of all the human race. With those brief but earth-shattering events, the future had been unveiled, and everything looked different as a result.

In particular, now that we have glimpsed in Jesus the way things are actually going to be – a new world created and nurtured by God's generous, self-giving love and grace – we can see how we should live in the present. If the future is shaped by saving grace, then the present must anticipate that. The world is full of destructive ways of living, in which people turn their backs on God and act according to whatever passion is sweeping them along. That's no way to prepare for God's grace-filled future. Rather, as verse 13 puts it, those who wait eagerly for Jesus to appear, the Jesus who is not only king and saviour but the living embodiment of God himself, must lead lives which can be summed up in three words.

First, sober. You are a real human being, so don't diminish your humanness by drunkenness or other kinds of behaviour that make you more like an irrational animal. You are a creature designed to find fulfilment in being generous and kind to others; drunkenness and similar behaviour results first in your being selfish (the drunk isn't really interested in anybody else but his or her own self) and then in your being harmful to your own self in turn.

Second, just. The Christian who understands what God's grace is all about – the powerful love which will turn the world the right way up, and has begun to do so in Jesus – will not be able to stand idly by and watch injustice at work. The word 'righteous', which is sometimes used as a translation here, captures one element of this – that justice must be a principle at work in one's own life as well – but often sounds negative (as in 'self-righteous'). The word Paul uses is a profoundly positive one, and designates a life that has been both put to rights itself and is devoted to working so that the world may be put to rights as well.

Third, devout. The last century or so in the Western world has seen a heavy reaction against the piety, and perhaps the pietism, of former generations. All you have to do is to suggest the long faces, the upturned eyes, the hushed tones of an imaginary Victorian church or home, and people at once think, 'Oh! I don't want to be like that.' But genuine piety, true devotion, needs none of those affectations. Of course, when people are learning to pray and to live in the light of God's love for the first time, they will often feel strange in doing so, and that strangeness may show in their face, voice and bearing. Like someone beginning to learn a musical instrument, they may quite unintentionally find themselves making odd faces as they do so. But someone who is devout in a mature way is someone who, at ease with themselves and able to put others equally at their ease, regards it as natural and normal to be in God's presence, to pray, and to live in such a way as to anticipate the future final appearing of Jesus.

At this point people may come up with another objection. It all sounds much too hard. The old habits of life are too strong. Paul is ready for this objection, and answers it in verse 14. Jesus isn't telling us to live in an impossible way. He is welcoming us into a way of life for which he has set us free. His own death on our behalf has unlocked the door of ethical possibilities, and we are now invited to go through into his new world, the world of genuine purity, the world where we can begin to contribute positively to people and society around us. That, by the way, is the normal meaning of 'good works' in verse 14; we might understand the phrase simply as 'behaving yourself', but both here and in 3.1, 3.8 and 3.14 it refers to generous and helpful actions on behalf of the wider community.

We must assume, then, that Titus isn't simply supposed to insist on certain styles of behaviour for their own sake, or to exhort or warn people by the sheer force of his own personality. The way he is to insist on all this (verse 15) is, as Paul himself has done, to explain to people how their present life relates to God's future, and to encourage them to make that future their own here and now.

TITUS 3.1–8a

God's Kindness and Generosity – and Ours

¹Remind them to submit to rulers and authorities, to be obedient, to be ready for every good work. ²They are not to speak evil of anyone, nor to be quarrelsome, but to be kindly. They must be completely gentle with everyone.

³We ourselves, you see, used at one time to be foolish, disobedient, deceived, and enslaved to various kinds of passions and pleasures. We spent our time in wickedness and jealousy. We were despicable in ourselves, and we hated one another. ⁴But when the kindness and generous love of God our saviour appeared, ⁵he saved us, not by works that we did in righteousness, but in accordance with his own mercy, through the washing of the new birth and the renewal of the holy spirit, ⁶which was poured out richly upon us through Jesus the Messiah, our saviour, ⁷so that we might be justified by his grace and be made his heirs, in accordance with the hope of the life of the age to come. ⁸The saying is sure.

I went to a spectacular birthday party last weekend. Our host, who was turning 70, had laid on a lavish evening. Nothing had been spared to make his guests comfortable and happy. The food was terrific; the wine of the highest class; each guest received a special little present; the music and other entertainment kept us all excited and cheerful. At the end there were fireworks. We departed into the night filled with the warmth that comes from someone else's lavish generosity.

But supposing all the guests at the party were people who, not long before, had been critical of the host, or had plotted to do him down in his business, or had been the kind of people who never enjoyed parties, who didn't realize when someone was trying to be generous to them, and who certainly weren't used to saying 'thank you'. Supposing, nevertheless, the host was determined to be generous, even to them. Why, you may ask, would anyone invite a bunch of miserable guests like that? Well, that's the question that faces us in this passage; because this, it appears, is precisely what God has done. And now he wants us to learn by his example.

Paul returns to the point he has made once or twice before in this letter. With Jesus, and the **gospel** message concerning him, something has been unveiled before the world. That something is nothing other than God's own kindness and loving goodness, which is so lavish that he has specifically not invited to his party people who were already the obvious guests, well qualified by their holiness of life to celebrate in his presence. Paul would insist, actually, that no such people existed; he himself was as well qualified as any (see, for instance, Philippians

115

3.2–6), but when he describes himself and his fellow Christians in verse 3 it's not a pretty sight. Under the calm surface of pious religious behaviour and observance there was a seething, crawling mass of lusts and desires, distorting his mind and heart and leading him into angry, hateful behaviour. Not the sort of person, after all, you'd expect God to invite to his party.

But that's the point, as so often in the New Testament. God's action in Jesus **Christ** is not a reward for good work already done. It's an act of free kindness and loving goodness (verse 4). And it results, not in a pat on the back because we're already the sort of people God wanted on his side, but in *washing* and *renewal*.

This is the one place in all Paul's letters where he talks about the 'new birth', which is familiar to many people from the third chapter of John's gospel, but which, apart from the present passage, hardly occurs at all in other early Christian writings. The main thing he says about it here is that it's God's free gift, and that it involves being made clean from everything which had previously polluted us. The reference to 'washing' is almost certainly intended, and most early Christians would have heard it like this, as a reference to **baptism** itself. As we know from Romans 6 and Colossians 3, Paul saw baptism as the moment when someone was brought into the community marked by the death and **resurrection** of Jesus. From 1 Corinthians 12 we learn that it is intimately connected, as well, with the gift of the **holy spirit**. These two seem to come together in the present passage, brief though the reference is.

Up to this point Paul had spoken of the 'appearing' of God's salvation in terms of the future arriving in the present and creating a new world for us to live in. This time, however, he wants to highlight *the effect on us* of the 'appearing' of God's kindness and goodness. It isn't just that we've glimpsed the future and discovered that it's full of God's grace. We are invited to look at our own selves, if we are baptized and believing members of Jesus' extended family, and to take stock of the radical change that God has accomplished in us. (If we are tempted to say, 'What radical change?', then either we were always so saintly that we never needed one – which Paul himself would doubt! – or we are so far from understanding his gospel that we hardly seem to have started on the road.) What we see, in a life transformed by the gospel, is the direct result of God's lavish, generous love. *And that's why he wants us to be generous, kind and gentle in turn.*

That's the point of verse 2. It's not just that God has decided to set up some new rules, for the sake of it, and that one of them happens to be that Christians should be nice to people. The reason for the early Christian rule of life is always more deep rooted than that. The reason we are summoned to avoid speaking evil of people, not to be quarrelsome and so on, is that we are ourselves the creatures of God's generous love, and if we aren't showing that same generous, kindly, forgiving love, we have obviously forgotten the path by which we've come.

This works at two different levels. At the first, our obligation to be kind and gentle to others is simply our response to God's love. We owe him our very lives; is it too much to ask that we respond gratefully by behaving in the way which brings him honour? But, at the second level, we discover with a shock that when we are kind and gentle to people *this itself is part of the 'appearing' of God's kindness and loving goodness.* God wants to continue the work of self-revelation he began in and through Jesus; and one of the primary ways he does this is by his followers acting in such a way that people will realize who God is and what he's like. The creator of the world is a lavish host, who has sent out a worldwide invitation to his party. We, as his messengers, must live in such a way that people will want to turn up.

TITUS 3.8b–15

Watch Out for Disputes and Divisions

^{8b}I want you to insist on these things, so that those who have put their faith in God may take care to be energetic in good works. Such things are good and profitable for people. ⁹But stay well clear of foolish disputes, genealogies, quarrels and squabbles about the law; they serve no purpose, and are worthless. ¹⁰If someone is causing divisions, give them a first warning, then a second, and then avoid them. ¹¹You know that a person like that is twisted, sinful and self-condemned.

¹²When I send Artemas to you, or maybe Tychicus, do your best to come to me at Nicopolis. That's where I've decided to spend the winter. ¹³Give a really good send-off to Zenas the lawyer and Apollos; make sure they don't go short of anything. ¹⁴All our people must learn to busy themselves with good works, so that they may meet any urgent needs that arise, and not be unfruitful.

¹⁵All the people with me send you their greetings. Greet those who love us in faith. Grace be with you all.

We received a charming wedding invitation today. In it, the young couple, both of whom are already working full time in the church, insisted that they didn't want ordinary presents. Instead, they urged guests who wanted to do so to make a donation to a particular charity which works with families, schools, hospitals and the like in severely deprived parts of the world. It's a fine idea – I hope it doesn't mean that the couple end up with no crockery and cutlery! – and it will do a great deal of good.

It is, in fact, a twenty-first-century way of doing what Paul is doing in verses 8 and 14: urging Titus to insist that Christians should 'be energetic in good works'. As we saw earlier, and as becomes clear in verse 14 in particular, the 'good works' in question are not 'living a good moral life' or 'obeying the **law**'. They are the 'good works' of giving practical help, particularly money, to those in need, or where there are social emergencies that require urgent assistance. This passage begins to sound, in fact, as though Titus is to set up what we today would call a charity organization.

In a sense, that's exactly what early Christianity was. One of the remarkable things the early Christians were known for – and one of the reasons for the rapid spread of the **faith** – is the way they were unstoppable when it came to helping others, both financially and in practical ways. If people were ill, they would nurse them. If they were hungry, they would get them food. If they were in prison, they would visit them. And so on. Not only with their own family – most people in the world would do that – but with strangers, with people from different ethnic groups, even with former enemies. This, of course, follows directly from the previous passage. Having been gripped by the generous love of God themselves, they couldn't help acting in the same way.

A further motive arises for insisting that people should busy themselves in this way: they must not be unfruitful (verse 14). An unfruitful Christian is like an unfruitful apple tree. It may look fine from time to time, but it isn't doing its job. Of course, there are many ways of bearing fruit. Not everyone can help in the same way. For some, staying at home and praying is the only thing, but in any case one of the best things, they can do. For others, prayer can and should pass into action.

When the church needs hard work and generous action, it's interesting how some people, perhaps as an avoidance technique, suddenly discover that there are all sorts of theological and biblical disputes that they need to hide behind. There is, of course, such a thing as worthwhile discussion of serious topics in the Bible and theology; I am the last person to deny that! But sometimes such discussions can take a turn for the worse, and become what Paul here calls 'foolish disputes' (verse 9). Sometimes, as he says, these concern genealogies. I was once lecturing to a group of Christian students, and afterwards several of them came up to me individually and asked me about the difference between the genealogies in Matthew's first chapter and Luke's third one. (I hadn't been lecturing on anything to do with them.) Clearly some people were anxious about what these passages implied for their view of scripture. Equally clearly, there were far more important things for intelligent young Christians to be thinking about.

Or it may be disputes about the law – not, presumably, questions about Christian behaviour, but rather about how to interpret the Jewish law from a Christian point of view. This is a serious subject and deserves careful study; but sometimes that study is overtaken by people with fixed views and a determination to foist them on other people. Most Christian teachers will know what it feels like to come away from such a discussion thinking that it would have been better to spend the evening digging the garden.

No pastor will want to leave it there. We all hope and pray that, however awkward someone may be, however many unnecessary tangles they get themselves and others into with their strange and convoluted ideas, we may be able to work with them, pray with them and help them to see a fuller and more rounded picture of Christian truth. But Paul, with all his own pastoral experience behind him, knows that that won't always be the case. The alternative is to do what Jesus recommended in Matthew 18, in relation to people who offend within the community: a first warning, then a second, then have nothing more to do with them.

We are, I suspect, shocked at this. We have lived for a long time, at least in the churches of the West, with the polar opposite, where almost everyone bends over backwards to be nice to almost everyone, and people who are causing trouble and division in the church often get away with it scot free. Sadly, there are people to whom the epithets 'twisted, sinful and self-condemned' apply only too well. Sometimes the only thing we can realistically do with them is to avoid them.

Paul's travel plans leave us, once more, fascinated but frustrated. The best-known 'Nicopolis' is on the western coast of Greece, and it's not clear when Paul might have gone there or why he would have expected Titus to leave Crete and join him there, some distance away. Maybe, though, we are meant to envisage Paul leaving Crete on his final voyage, intending to get to Nicopolis before winter and go on from there to Rome in the spring. That would have been quite a normal journey. In that case, as we know from Acts, the strong Mediterranean winds took a hand and blew his plans to bits.

One way or another, though, Paul always knew his plans were liable to be turned inside out and upside down. He had learned to roll with the punches. What mattered was not what happened to him, but the love, faith and grace that he cannot help mentioning once more as this gem of pastoral wisdom draws to its close.

GLOSSARY

the accuser, *see* the satan

age to come, *see* present age

apostle, disciple, the Twelve
'Apostle' means 'one who is sent'. It could be used of an ambassador or official delegate. In the New Testament it is sometimes used specifically of Jesus' inner circle of twelve; but Paul sees not only himself but several others outside the Twelve as 'apostles', the criterion being whether the person had personally seen the risen Jesus. Jesus' own choice of twelve close associates symbolized his plan to renew God's people, Israel; after the death of Judas Iscariot (Matthew 27.5; Acts 1.18), Matthias was chosen by lot to take his place, preserving the symbolic meaning. During Jesus' lifetime they, and many other followers, were seen as his 'disciples', which means 'pupils' or 'apprentices'.

baptism
Literally, 'plunging' people into water. From within a wider Jewish tradition of ritual washings and bathings, **John the Baptist** undertook a vocation of baptizing people in the Jordan, not as one ritual among others but as a unique moment of **repentance**, preparing them for the coming of the **kingdom of God**. Jesus himself was baptized by John, identifying himself with this renewal movement and developing it in his own way. His followers in turn baptized others. After his **resurrection**, and the sending of the **holy spirit**, baptism became the normal sign and means of entry into the community of Jesus' people. As early as Paul it was aligned both with the **Exodus** from Egypt (1 Corinthians 10.2) and with Jesus' death and resurrection (Romans 6.2–11).

Christ, *see* Messiah

circumcision, circumcised
The cutting off of the foreskin. Male circumcision was a major mark of identity for Jews, following its initial commandment to Abraham (Genesis 17), reinforced by Joshua (Joshua 5.2–9). Other peoples, e.g. the Egyptians, also circumcised male children. A line of thought from Deuteronomy (e.g. 30.6), through Jeremiah (e.g. 31.33), to the **Dead Sea Scrolls** and the New Testament (e.g. Romans 2.29) speaks of 'circumcision of the heart' as God's real desire, by which one may become inwardly what the male Jew is outwardly, that is, marked out as part

121

of God's people. At periods of Jewish assimilation into the surrounding culture, some Jews tried to remove the marks of circumcision (e.g. 1 Maccabees 1.11–15).

covenant

At the heart of Jewish belief is the conviction that the one God, YHWH, who had made the whole world, had called Abraham and his family to belong to him in a special way. The promises God made to Abraham and his family, and the requirements that were laid on them as a result, came to be seen in terms either of the agreement that a king would make with a subject people, or sometimes of the marriage bond between husband and wife. One regular way of describing this relationship was 'covenant', which can thus include both promise and **law**. The covenant was renewed at Mount Sinai with the giving of the **Torah**; in Deuteronomy before the entry to the promised land; and, in a more focused way, with David (e.g. Psalm 89). Jeremiah 31 promised that after the punishment of **exile** God would make a 'new covenant' with his people, forgiving them and binding them to him more intimately. Jesus believed that this was coming true through his **kingdom**-proclamation and his death and **resurrection**. The early Christians developed these ideas in various ways, believing that in Jesus the promises had at last been fulfilled.

Dead Sea Scrolls

A collection of texts, some in remarkably good repair, some extremely fragmentary, found in the late 1940s around Qumran (near the north-east corner of the Dead Sea), and virtually all now edited, translated and in the public domain. They formed all or part of the library of a strict monastic group, most likely Essenes, founded in the mid-second century BC and lasting until the Jewish – Roman war of 66–70. The scrolls include the earliest existing manuscripts of the Hebrew and Aramaic scriptures, and several other important documents of community regulations, scriptural exegesis, hymns, wisdom writings, and other literature. They shed a flood of light on one small segment within the Judaism of Jesus' day, helping us to understand how some Jews at least were thinking, praying and reading scripture. Despite attempts to prove the contrary, they make no reference to **John the Baptist**, Jesus, Paul, James or early Christianity in general.

disciple, *see* apostle

eucharist

The meal in which the earliest Christians, and Christians ever since, obeyed Jesus' command to 'do this in remembrance of him' at the Last Supper (Luke 22.19; 1 Corinthians 11.23–26). The word 'eucharist' itself comes from the Greek for 'thanksgiving'; it means, basically, 'the thank-you meal', and looks back to the many times when Jesus took bread, gave thanks for it, broke it and gave it to people (e.g. Luke 24.30; John 6.11). Other early phrases for the same meal are 'the Lord's Supper' (1 Corinthians 11.20) and 'the breaking of bread' (Acts 2.42). Later it came to be called 'the mass' (from the Latin word at the end of the service, meaning 'sent out') and 'holy communion' (Paul speaks of 'sharing' or 'communion' in the body and blood of Christ). Later theological controversies about the precise meaning of the various actions and elements of the meal should not obscure its centrality in earliest Christian living and its continuing vital importance today.

exile

Deuteronomy (29—30) warned that if Israel disobeyed YHWH, he would send his people into exile, but that if they then repented he would bring them back. When the Babylonians sacked Jerusalem and took the people into exile, prophets such as Jeremiah interpreted this as the fulfilment of this prophecy, and made further promises about how long exile would last (70 years, according to Jeremiah 25.12; 29.10). Sure enough, exiles began to return in the late sixth century (Ezra 1.1). However, the post-exilic period was largely a disappointment, since the people were still enslaved to foreigners (Nehemiah 9.36); and at the height of persecution by the Syrians, Daniel 9.2, 24 spoke of the 'real' exile lasting not for 70 years but for 70 *weeks* of years, i.e., 490 years. Longing for the real 'return from exile', when the prophecies of Isaiah, Jeremiah, etc. would be fulfilled, and redemption from pagan oppression accomplished, continued to characterize many Jewish movements, and was a major theme in Jesus' proclamation and his summons to **repentance**.

Exodus

The Exodus from Egypt took place, according to the book of that name, under the leadership of Moses, after long years in which the Israelites had been enslaved there. (According to Genesis 15.13f., this was itself part of God's covenanted promise to Abraham.) It demonstrated, to them and to Pharaoh, King of Egypt, that Israel was God's special child (Exodus 4.22). They then wandered through the Sinai wilderness for 40 years, led by God in a pillar of cloud and fire; early on in this time they were given the **Torah** on Mount Sinai itself. Finally, after the death of Moses and under the leadership of Joshua, they crossed the Jordan and entered, and eventually conquered, the promised land of Canaan. This event, commemorated annually in Passover and other Jewish festivals, gave the Israelites not only a powerful memory of what had made them a people, but also a particular shape and content to their faith in YHWH as not only creator but also redeemer; and in subsequent enslavements, particularly the **exile**, they looked for a further redemption which would be, in effect, a new Exodus. Probably no other past event so dominated the imagination of first-century Jews; among them the early Christians, following the lead of Jesus himself, continually referred back to the Exodus to give meaning and shape to their own critical events, most particularly Jesus' death and **resurrection**.

faith

Faith in the New Testament covers a wide area of human trust and trustworthiness, merging into love at one end of the scale and loyalty at the other. Within

Jewish and Christian thinking faith in God also includes *belief*, accepting certain things as true about God, and what he has done in the world (e.g. bringing Israel out of Egypt; raising Jesus from the dead). For Jesus, 'faith' often seems to mean 'recognizing that God is decisively at work to bring the **kingdom** through Jesus'. For Paul, 'faith' is both the specific belief that Jesus is Lord and that God raised him from the dead (Romans 10.9) and the response of grateful human love to sovereign divine love (Galatians 2.20). This faith is, for Paul, the solitary badge of membership in God's people in **Christ**, marking them out in a way that **Torah**, and the works it prescribes, can never do.

Gentiles

The Jews divided the world into Jews and non-Jews. The Hebrew word for non-Jews, *goyim*, carries overtones both of family identity (i.e., not of Jewish ancestry) and of worship (i.e. of idols, not of the one true God YHWH). Though many Jews established good relations with Gentiles, not least in the Jewish Diaspora (the dispersion of Jews away from Palestine), officially there were taboos against contact such as intermarriage. In the New Testament the Greek word *ethne*, 'nations', carries the same meanings as *goyim*. Part of Paul's overmastering agenda was to insist that Gentiles who believed in Jesus had full rights in the Christian community alongside believing Jews, without having to become **circumcised**.

good news, gospel, message, word

The idea of 'good news', for which an older English word is 'gospel', had two principal meanings for first-century Jews. First, with roots in Isaiah, it meant the news of YHWH's long-awaited victory over evil and rescue of his people. Second, it was used in the Roman world of the accession, or birthday, or the emperor. Since for Jesus and Paul the announcement of God's inbreaking **kingdom** was both the fulfilment of prophecy and a challenge to the world's present rulers, 'gospel' became an important shorthand for both the message of Jesus himself, and the apostolic message about him. Paul saw this message as itself the vehicle of God's saving power (Romans 1.16; 1 Thessalonians 2.13).

The four canonical 'gospels' tell the story of Jesus in such a way as to bring out both these aspects (unlike some other so-called 'gospels' circulated in the second and subsequent centuries, which tended both to cut off the scriptural and Jewish roots of Jesus' achievement and to inculcate a private spirituality rather than confrontation with the world's rulers). Since in Isaiah this creative, life-giving good news was seen as God's own powerful word (40.8; 55.11), the early Christians could use 'word' or 'message' as another shorthand for the basic Christian proclamation.

gospel, *see* good news

heaven

Heaven is God's dimension of the created order (Genesis 1.1; Psalm 115.16; Matthew 6.9), whereas 'earth' is the world of space, time and matter that we know.

'Heaven' thus sometimes stands, reverentially, for 'God' (as in Matthew's regular '**kingdom of heaven**'). Normally hidden from human sight, heaven is occasionally revealed or unveiled so that people can see God's dimension of ordinary life (e.g. 2 Kings 6.17; Revelation 1, 4—5). Heaven in the New Testament is thus not usually seen as the place where God's people go after death; at the end the New Jerusalem descends *from* heaven *to* earth, joining the two dimensions for ever. 'Entering the kingdom of heaven' does not mean 'going to heaven after death', but belonging in the present to the people who steer their earthly course by the standards and purposes of heaven (cf. the Lord's Prayer: 'on earth as in heaven', Matthew 6.10) and who are assured of membership in the **age to come**.

Herodians

Herod the Great ruled Judaea from 37 to 4 BC; after his death his territory was divided between his sons Archelaus, Herod Antipas (the Herod of the **gospels**), and Philip. The Herodians supported the claims of Antipas to be the true king of the Jews. Though the **Pharisees** would normally oppose such a claim, they could make common cause with the Herodians when facing a common threat (e.g. Jesus, Mark 3.6).

high priest, *see* priests

holy spirit

In Genesis 1.2, the spirit is God's presence and power *within* creation, without God being identified with creation. The same spirit entered people, notably the prophets, enabling them to speak and act for God. At his **baptism** by **John the Baptist**, Jesus was specially equipped with the spirit, resulting in his remarkable public career (Acts 10.38). After his **resurrection**, his followers were themselves filled (Acts 2) by the same spirit, now identified as Jesus' own spirit: the creator God was acting afresh, remaking the world and them too. The spirit enabled them to live out a holiness which the **Torah** could not, producing 'fruit' in their lives, giving them 'gifts' with which to serve God, the world and the church, and assuring them of future resurrection (Romans 8; Galatians 4—5; 1 Corinthians 12—14). From very early in Christianity (e.g. Galatians 4.1–7), the spirit became part of the new revolutionary definition of God himself: 'the one who sends the son and the spirit of the son'.

John (the Baptist)

Jesus' cousin on his mother's side, born a few months before Jesus; his father was a **priest**. He acted as a prophet, baptizing in the Jordan – dramatically re-enacting the **Exodus** from Egypt – to prepare people, by **repentance**, for God's coming judgment. He may have had some contact with the Essenes, though his eventual public message was different from theirs. Jesus' own vocation was decisively confirmed at his **baptism** by John. As part of John's message of the **kingdom**, he outspokenly criticized Herod Antipas for marrying his brother's wife. Herod had him imprisoned, and then beheaded him at his wife's request

(Mark 6.14–29). Groups of John's disciples continued a separate existence, without merging into Christianity, for some time afterwards (e.g. Acts 19.1–7).

justification

God's declaration, from his position as judge of all the world, that someone is in the right, despite universal sin. This declaration will be made on the last day on the basis of an entire life (Romans 2.1–16), but is brought forward into the present on the basis of Jesus' achievement, because sin has been dealt with through his cross (Romans 3.21—4.25); the means of this present justification is simply **faith**. This means, particularly, that Jews and **Gentiles** alike are full members of the family promised by God to Abraham (Galatians 3; Romans 4).

kingdom of God, kingdom of heaven

Best understood as the king*ship*, or sovereign and saving rule, of Israel's God YHWH, as celebrated in several psalms (e.g. 99.1) and prophecies (e.g. Daniel 6.26f.). Because YHWH was the creator God, when he finally became king in the way he intended this would involve setting the world to rights, and particularly rescuing Israel from its enemies. 'Kingdom of God' and various equivalents (e.g. 'No king but God!') became a revolutionary slogan around the time of Jesus. Jesus' own announcement of God's kingdom redefined these expectations around his own very different plan and vocation. His invitation to people to 'enter' the kingdom was a way of summoning them to allegiance to himself and his programme, seen as the start of God's long-awaited saving reign. For Jesus, the kingdom was coming not in a single move, but in stages, of which his own public career was one, his death and **resurrection** another, and a still future consummation another. Note that 'kingdom of **heaven**' is Matthew's preferred form for the same phrase, following a regular Jewish practice of saying 'heaven' rather than 'God'. It does not refer to a place ('heaven'), but to the fact of God's becoming king in and through Jesus and his achievement. Paul speaks of Jesus, as **Messiah**, already in possession of his kingdom, waiting to hand it over finally to the father (1 Corinthians 15.23–28; cf. Ephesians 5.5).

law, *see* **Torah**

life, soul, spirit

Ancient people held many different views about what made human beings the special creatures they are. Some, including many Jews, believed that to be complete, humans needed bodies as well as inner selves. Others, including many influenced by the philosophy of Plato (fourth century BC), believed that the important part of a human was the 'soul' (Gk: *psyche*), which at death would be happily freed from its bodily prison. Confusingly for us, the same word *psyche* is often used in the New Testament within a Jewish framework where it clearly means 'life' or 'true self', without implying a body/soul dualism that devalues the body. Human inwardness of experience and understanding can also be referred to as 'spirit'. *See also* **resurrection**.

message, *see* good news

Messiah, messianic, Christ

The Hebrew word means literally 'anointed one', hence in theory either a prophet, **priest** or king. In Greek this translates as *Christos*; 'Christ' in early Christianity was a title, and only gradually became an alternative proper name for Jesus. In practice 'Messiah' is mostly restricted to the notion, which took various forms in ancient Judaism, of the coming king who would be David's true heir, through whom YHWH would bring judgment to the world, and in particular would rescue Israel from pagan enemies. There was no single template of expectations. Scriptural stories and promises contributed to different ideals and movements, often focused on (a) decisive military defeat of Israel's enemies and (b) rebuilding or cleansing the **Temple**. The **Dead Sea Scrolls** speak of two 'Messiahs', one a priest and the other a king. The universal early Christian belief that Jesus was Messiah is only explicable, granted his crucifixion by the Romans (which would have been seen as a clear sign that he was not the Messiah), by their belief that God had raised him from the dead, so vindicating the implicit messianic claims of his earlier ministry.

miracles

Like some of the old prophets, notably Elijah and Elisha, Jesus performed many deeds of remarkable power, particularly healings. The **gospels** refer to these as 'deeds of power', 'signs', 'marvels' or 'paradoxes'. Our word 'miracle' tends to imply that God, normally 'outside' the closed system of the world, sometimes 'intervenes'; miracles have then frequently been denied as a matter of principle. However, in the Bible God is always present, however strangely, and 'deeds of power' are seen as *special* acts of a *present* God rather than as *intrusive* acts of an *absent* one. Jesus' own 'mighty works' are seen particularly, following prophecy, as evidence of his messiahship (e.g. Matthew 11.2–6).

Mishnah

The main codification of Jewish law (**Torah**) by the **rabbis**, produced in about AD 200, reducing to writing the 'oral Torah' which in Jesus' day ran parallel to the 'written Torah'. The Mishnah is itself the basis of the much larger collections of traditions in the two Talmuds (roughly AD 400).

parables

From the Old Testament onwards, prophets and other teachers used various storytelling devices as vehicles for their challenge to Israel (e.g. 2 Samuel 12.1–7). Sometimes these appeared as visions with interpretations (e.g. Daniel 7). Similar techniques were used by the **rabbis**. Jesus made his own creative adaptation of these traditions, in order to break open the world-view of his contemporaries and to invite them to share his vision of God's **kingdom** instead. His stories portrayed this as something that was *happening*, not just a timeless truth, and enabled his hearers to step inside the story and make it their own. As with some Old Testament visions, some of Jesus' parables have their own interpretations (e.g. the sower, Mark 4); others are thinly disguised retellings of the prophetic story of Israel (e.g. the wicked tenants, Mark 12).

parousia

Literally, it means 'presence', as opposed to 'absence', and is sometimes used by Paul with this sense (e.g. Philippians 2.12). It was already used in the Roman world for the ceremonial arrival of, for example, the emperor at a subject city or colony. Although the ascended Lord is not 'absent' from the church, when he 'appears' (Colossians 3.4; 1 John 3.2) in his 'second coming' this will be, in effect, an 'arrival' like that of the emperor, and Paul uses it thus in 1 Corinthians 15.23; 1 Thessalonians 2.19; etc. In the **gospels** it is found only in Matthew 24 (verses 3, 27, 39).

Pharisees, lawyers, legal experts, rabbis

The Pharisees were an unofficial but powerful Jewish pressure group through most of the first centuries BC and AD. Largely lay-led, though including some **priests**, their aim was to purify Israel through intensified observance of the Jewish law (**Torah**), developing their own traditions about the precise meaning and application of scripture, their own patterns of prayer and other devotion, and their own calculations of the national hope. Though not all legal experts were Pharisees, most Pharisees were thus legal experts.

They effected a democratization of Israel's life, since for them the study and practice of Torah was equivalent to worshipping in the **Temple** – though they were adamant in pressing their own rules for the Temple liturgy on an unwilling (and often **Sadducean**) priesthood. This enabled them to survive AD 70 and, merging into the early rabbinic movement, to develop new ways forward. Politically they stood up for ancestral traditions, and were at the forefront of various movements of revolt against both pagan overlordship and compromised Jewish leaders. By Jesus' day there were two distinct schools, the stricter one of Shammai, more inclined towards armed revolt, and the more lenient one of Hillel, ready to live and let live.

Jesus' debates with the Pharisees are at least as much a matter of agenda and policy (Jesus strongly opposed their separatist nationalism) as about details of theology and piety. Saul of Tarsus was a fervent right-wing Pharisee, presumably a Shammaite, until his conversion.

After the disastrous war of AD 66–70, these schools of Hillel and Shammai continued bitter debate on appropriate policy. Following the further disaster of AD 135 (the failed Bar-Kochba revolt against Rome) their traditions were carried on by the rabbis who, though looking to the earlier Pharisees for inspiration, developed a Torah-piety in which personal holiness and purity took the place of political agendas.

present age, age to come, the life of God's coming age

By the time of Jesus many Jewish thinkers divided history into two periods: 'the present age' and 'the age to come' – the latter being the time when YHWH would at last act decisively to judge evil, to rescue Israel, and to create a new world of justice and peace. The early Christians believed that, though the full blessings of the coming age lay still in the future, it had already begun with Jesus, particularly with his death and **resurrection**, and that by **faith** and **baptism** they were able to enter it already. For this reason, the customary translation 'eternal life' is rendered here as 'the life of God's coming age'.

priests, high priest

Aaron, the older brother of Moses, was appointed Israel's first high priest (Exodus 28—29), and in theory his descendants were Israel's priests thereafter. Other members of his tribe (Levi) were 'Levites', performing other liturgical duties but not sacrificing. Priests lived among the people all around the country, having a local teaching role (Leviticus 10.11; Malachi 2.7), and going to Jerusalem by rotation to perform the **Temple** liturgy (e.g. Luke 2.8).

David appointed Zadok (whose Aaronic ancestry is sometimes questioned) as high priest, and his family remained thereafter the senior priests in Jerusalem, probably the ancestors of the **Sadducees**. One explanation of the origins of the Qumran Essenes is that they were a dissident group who believed themselves to be the rightful chief priests.

rabbis, *see* Pharisees

repentance

Literally, this means 'turning back'. It is widely used in the Old Testament and subsequent Jewish literature to indicate both a personal turning away from sin and Israel's corporate turning away from idolatry and back to YHWH. Through both meanings, it is linked to the idea of 'return from **exile**'; if Israel is to 'return' in all senses, it must 'return' to YHWH. This is at the heart of the summons of both **John the Baptist** and Jesus. In Paul's writings it is mostly used for **Gentiles** turning away from idols to serve the true God; also for sinning Christians who need to return to Jesus.

resurrection

In most biblical thought, human bodies matter and are not merely disposable prisons for the **soul**. When ancient Israelites wrestled with the goodness and justice of YHWH, the creator, they ultimately came to insist that he must raise the dead (Isaiah 26.19; Daniel 12.2–3) – a suggestion firmly resisted by classical pagan thought. The longed-for return from **exile** was also spoken of in terms of YHWH raising dry bones to new **life** (Ezekiel 37.1–14). These ideas were developed in the second-**Temple** period, not least at times of martyrdom (e.g.

2 Maccabees 7). Resurrection was not just 'life after death', but a newly embodied life *after* 'life after death'; those at present dead were either 'asleep', or seen as 'souls', 'angels' or 'spirits', awaiting new embodiment.

The early Christian belief that Jesus had been raised from the dead was not that he had 'gone to **heaven**', or that he had been 'exalted', or was 'divine'; they believed all those as well, but each could have been expressed without mention of resurrection. Only the bodily resurrection of Jesus explains the rise of the early church, particularly its belief in Jesus' messiahship (which his crucifixion would have called into question). The early Christians believed that they themselves would be raised to a new, transformed bodily life at the time of the Lord's return or **parousia** (e.g. Philippians 3.20f.).

sabbath

The Jewish sabbath, the seventh day of the week, was a regular reminder both of creation (Genesis 2.3; Exodus 20.8–11) and of the **Exodus** (Deuteronomy 5.15). Along with **circumcision** and the food laws, it was one of the badges of Jewish identity within the pagan world of late antiquity, and a considerable body of Jewish **law** and custom grew up around its observance.

sacrifice

Like all ancient people, the Israelites offered animal and vegetable sacrifices to their God. Unlike others, they possessed a highly detailed written code (mostly in Leviticus) for what to offer and how to offer it; this in turn was developed in the **Mishnah** (*c.* AD 200). The Old Testament specifies that sacrifices can only be offered in the Jerusalem **Temple**; after this was destroyed in AD 70, sacrifices ceased, and Judaism developed further the idea, already present in some teachings, of prayer, fasting and almsgiving as alternative forms of sacrifice. The early Christians used the language of sacrifice in connection with such things as holiness, evangelism and the **eucharist**.

Sadducees

By Jesus' day, the Sadducees were the aristocracy of Judaism, possibly tracing their origins to the family of Zadok, David's **high priest**. Based in Jerusalem, and including most of the leading priestly families, they had their own traditions and attempted to resist the pressure of the **Pharisees** to conform to theirs. They claimed to rely only on the Pentateuch (the first five books of the Old Testament), and denied any doctrine of a future life, particularly of the **resurrection** and other ideas associated with it, presumably because of the encouragement such beliefs gave to revolutionary movements. No writings from the Sadducees have survived, unless the apocryphal book of Ben-Sirach ('Ecclesiasticus') comes from them. The Sadducees themselves did not survive the destruction of Jerusalem and the **Temple** in AD 70.

GLOSSARY

the satan, 'the accuser', demons

The Bible is never very precise about the identity of the figure known as 'the satan'. The Hebrew word means 'the accuser', and at times the satan seems to be a member of YHWH's heavenly council, with special responsibility as director of prosecutions (1 Chronicles 21.1; Job 1—2; Zechariah 3.1f.). However, it becomes identified variously with the serpent of the garden of Eden (Genesis 3.1–15) and with the rebellious daystar cast out of **heaven** (Isaiah 14.12–15), and was seen by many Jews as the quasi-personal source of evil standing behind both human wickedness and large-scale injustice, sometimes operating through semi-independent 'demons'. By Jesus' time various words were used to denote this figure, including Beelzebul/b (lit. 'Lord of the flies') and simply 'the evil one'; Jesus warned his followers against the deceits this figure could perpetrate. His opponents accused him of being in league with the satan, but the early Christians believed that Jesus in fact defeated it both in his own struggles with temptation (Matthew 4; Luke 4), his exorcisms of demons, and his death (1 Corinthians 2.8; Colossians 2.15). Final victory over this ultimate enemy is thus assured (Revelation 20), though the struggle can still be fierce for Christians (Ephesians 6.10–20).

soul, *see* life

spirit, *see* life, holy spirit

Temple

The Temple in Jerusalem was planned by David (*c.* 1000 BC) and built by his son Solomon as the central sanctuary for all Israel. After reforms under Hezekiah and Josiah in the seventh century BC, it was destroyed by Babylon in 587 BC. Rebuilding by the returned **exiles** began in 538 BC, and was completed in 516, initiating the 'second Temple period'. Judas Maccabaeus cleansed it in 164 BC after its desecration by Antiochus Epiphanes (167). Herod the Great began to rebuild and beautify it in 19 BC; the work was completed in AD 63. The Temple was destroyed by the Romans in AD 70. Many Jews believed it should and would be rebuilt; some still do. The Temple was not only the place of **sacrifice**; it was believed to be the unique dwelling of YHWH on earth, the place where **heaven** and earth met.

Torah, Jewish law

'Torah', narrowly conceived, consists of the first five books of the Old Testament, the 'five books of Moses' or 'Pentateuch'. (These contain much law, but also much narrative.) It can also be used for the whole Old Testament scriptures, though strictly these are the 'law, prophets and writings'. In a broader sense, it refers to the whole developing corpus of Jewish legal tradition, written and oral; the oral Torah was initially codified in the **Mishnah** around AD 200, with wider developments found in the two Talmuds, of Babylon and Jerusalem, codified around AD 400. Many Jews in the time of Jesus and Paul regarded the Torah as being so strongly God-given as to be almost itself, in some sense, divine; some (e.g. Ben Sirach 24) identified it with the figure of 'Wisdom'. Doing what Torah said was not seen as a means of earning God's favour, but rather of expressing gratitude, and as a key badge of Jewish identity.

word, *see* **good news**

YHWH

The ancient Israelite name for God, from at least the time of the **Exodus** (Exodus 6.2f.). It may originally have been pronounced 'Yahweh', but by the time of Jesus it was considered too holy to speak out loud, except for the **high priest** once a year in the Holy of Holies in the **Temple**. Instead, when reading scripture, pious Jews would say *Adonai*, 'Lord', marking this usage by adding the vowels of *Adonai* to the consonants of YHWH, eventually producing the hybrid 'Jehovah'. The word YHWH is formed from the verb 'to be', combining 'I am who I am', 'I will be who I will be', and perhaps 'I am because I am', emphasizing YHWH's sovereign creative power.

STUDY GUIDE

Introducing the Study

1 and 2 Timothy and Titus for Everyone is one in a series of commentaries written by N. T. Wright, noted Pauline and New Testament scholar, who intended these to be guides for readers ready to delve deeper into the scriptures. Suitable for group or individual study, Wright provides his own translation of the early Christian letters covered in this volume. Wright notes that 'these letters are very practical, offering encouragement and advice on the day-to-day life of a local church and the role of the chief pastor within it. At the same time, they constantly give us glimpses of a rich theological picture of Jesus, and of the power of the gospel' (page xii).

The commentary on each letter includes Wright's translation of the biblical text divided into small sections, accompanied by insights into its context and in-depth explanation of each segment. Notice that Wright provides a glossary for key words at the end of the volume. Your personal preparation for each session might include studying the selected texts in different translations as well as praying for guidance in understanding and relating those scriptures to your own life. Listen for the spirit's encouragement to you as you encounter the letters to early believers and churches, and recall Wright's reminder to us in the introduction: 'On the very first occasion when someone stood up in public to tell people about Jesus, he made it very clear: this message is for everyone.'

If Using the Guide for Individual Study

In addition to your copy of *1 and 2 Timothy and Titus for Everyone*, you may wish to read Wright's translations alongside other translations, which you can find online or perhaps in a local library. Did you study a language in school? Consider finding a copy of the New Testament in that language; the additional insights coming from the unfamiliarity of that language can be spiritually revealing. Completing the questions for each text in writing (never mind complete sentences; bullet points get full marks) and completing the suggested activities as if a good friend was by your side will enrich your experience.

If Using the Guide as a Group Member

- Be prepared by reading the scriptures before the sessions.
- Be on time for each session.
- Be encouraging to everyone.
- Be willing to contribute to group discussions.
- Be prayerful that great things will come from this study.

If Serving Others by Facilitating a Group

God bless you! This guide was prepared with you in mind, in the hope and prayer that spiritual blessings are abundant for you as well as those you lead. Every group is unique, so take this guide as a starting place, adapting and using the resources provided. Written for four one-hour sessions, you could adapt the length of your study to meet your needs. As an extra consideration, since these three letters are significantly different in length, this guide will explore them in order while arranging the sessions into manageable lengths. In addition, the last session concludes with a culminating activity session which covers all of the scriptures studied.

Suggested Session Format

Opening Prayer (1 minute)
Group Opening (5 minutes)
Exploring the Scriptures (30 minutes)
Applying the Scriptures (15 minutes)
Sharing 'Oh Wow' Moments (5 minutes)
Closing Prayer (1 minute)
Ticket Out the Door (3 minutes)

Readings for Each Session

Session One: 1 Timothy 1.1—3.16
Session Two: 1 Timothy 4.1—6.21
Session Three: 2 Timothy 1.1—4.22
Session Four: Titus 1.1—3.15

Helpful Hints for Facilitators

- Set up the room where you will meet early. Create expectations for learning by changing the usual appearance of the room. (Be sure to get permission before making any changes!)
- Ask others to lead a part of the session.

- Allow time for reflection. Silence may improve the quality of group responses.
- Involve as many persons as possible. Extend conversations by replying 'Yes, and . . .'
- Engage the group to reset the room to its original condition, building a sense of purpose for the group.
- Pray for the members individually and as a group. The message of these letters will change hearts and lives, as well as churches.

SESSION ONE: 1 TIMOTHY 1.1—3.16
INSTRUCTIONS FOR CHURCHES

(Pages 3–30)

Opening Prayer (1 minute)

King Jesus, our hope, teach us to read your word with discernment, to study your word diligently, and to live your word in grace, mercy and peace. Amen.

Group Opening (5 minutes)

Most of the letters contained in the New Testament were written to churches, but the three letters grouped together and called the Pastoral Letters were written to individuals. Paul is named as the writer of all three letters, and he writes to Timothy and Titus to instruct them in their own ministries. Wright notes that these three letters might well be known as 'the Teacher's Manual' because Paul describes the kind of teaching that Timothy and Titus should be doing, as well as the kind of teaching that others shouldn't do. The author examines some of the discussion around the authorship of these three letters and comes to the conclusion that the best thing for this book is to refer to the writer as Paul. These letters were written sometime between 50 and 100 AD and there is no way to determine in what order they were written.

Exploring the Scriptures (30 minutes)

These questions are intended to help you guide a group discussion of the first three chapters of 1 Timothy. There are likely more questions than you will have time to discuss, so feel free to use those which you think would most benefit the group you serve. The questions will also guide the individual reader in study.

1. On page 5, Wright suggests that we can detect two primary concerns running through 1 Timothy. What are those concerns? Are those concerns still issues in today's churches?

2. According to Wright, the Jewish law is like a map which only maps what?

3. How does Wright contrast the Jewish law and the law of new life which Paul describes in his letters?

4. Does Wright hold the position that the law is less important since the coming of Jesus and the developing role of Christian teaching?

5. Why, according to Wright, is Paul part of a pattern in which God uses unlikely people? What examples of this pattern have you observed in your own relationships?

6. 'In a world of suspicion, of lies and counter-lies, God's project to save the world is built on trust', Wright asserts (page 10). Write your understanding of this assertion in a single sentence and share it with others.

7. 'Fight the glorious battle, holding on to faith and a good conscience' is the direction Paul gives to the younger Timothy. How does a person develop a Christian conscience? What happens when conscience no longer plays a role in a Christian's life?

8. Paul names two men as examples of those who lose their way along the road to becoming Christian. What is the other reference to Hymenaeus, and how does it reflect on Paul's condemnation of him?

9. Wright translates 1 Timothy 1.20 as 'I have handed them over to the satan'. What does Wright mean by this? To learn more, go to the glossary and read the entry on 'satan'. How does Wright's treatment of that term fit into your previous understanding of that term?

10. In what context is Jeremiah 29.7 used in the discussion of 1 Timothy 2.1–7? What is the basis for Wright's explanation of how this passage might be interpreted?

11. Wright references 1 Corinthians 8.6 in his interpretation of 1 Timothy 2.5, stating 'it offers an astonishing redefinition of Jewish monotheism, with Jesus in the middle of it' (page 15). He then explains one way in which the old definition is maintained and another way in which it is different and new. Be prepared to explain which you think takes precedence and how the addition of Jesus expresses the idea of Christian monotheism.

12. N. T. Wright is a biblical interpreter who possesses great insight into scripture. He is acknowledged as a leading interpreter of Paul and the New Testament alike. Gifted as a scholar and living out

his call to minister to others, he is conservative in his approach to scholarship, as in the case of referring to the writer of this letter as Paul. He takes the Bible seriously as the word of God and as the pattern for Christian living. The next passage, 1 Timothy 2.8–15, is difficult to approach and to interpret. This may be a good time for us to pray! *Almighty God, we acknowledge that the scriptures we are about to study are difficult to understand and apply, and that persons of equal devotion to you and love for you who are deep in knowledge of your word do not interpret these scriptures in the same ways. Help us to glimpse the truth in these words and to regard one another in the love with which Jesus loves us. Where we are challenged in our beliefs, give us the grace to behave soberly, to study intently and to speak in the love which we share for you. Amen.*

13. Using a translation other than that provided by the author, ask someone to read this passage. Pay particular attention to 1 Timothy 2.12 'I do not permit a woman to teach or have authority over a man; she must be silent (NIV)'. Wright provides a commonly held interpretation in stating: 'The whole passage seems to be saying that women are second-class citizens. They aren't even allowed to dress prettily. They are the daughters of Eve, and she was the original troublemaker. The best thing for them to do is to get on, and have children, to behave themselves and to keep quiet'. Please notice that Wright will take a different approach and offer a different translation.

14. Wright acknowledges that some people will read his explanation and approach as accommodating a 'let's just get along' approach, a criticism which he denies.

15. On a large surface, large enough for all in the group to read, create the list which Wright introduces with the words 'it doesn't fit with what we see in the rest of the New Testament' on pages 17–18. The list should contain at least five items.

16. Wright points out that the key to understanding the entire passage is in recognizing that women should be allowed to study the Bible and not be restrained from doing so. The following words 'They should be in full submission' is most commonly understood as to 'men or their husbands', but that interpretation can also be understood as in their attitude as learners, submissive to the word of God. The word translated 'silence' in this passage typically means 'in quietness and in composure', and the word which is usually translated as 'complete silence' is a different word from the one present here.

17. Ephesus, the most likely location for Timothy's ministry, was the home to the Temple of Artemis (Roman-Diana), in which all of the

priestly roles were occupied by women. There is some thought that the female-dominated Temple of Artemis was influencing Christian practice in Ephesus and that Paul was writing to counter this influence.

18. In that context, then, Wright translates verse 12 in this way: 'I'm not saying that women should teach men, or try to dictate to them; rather, that they should be left undisturbed' (page 18). The guiding principle behind this interpretation seems to be that teachers should possess adequate training, knowledge and maturity before leading a church in Bible study.

19. The word 'overseeing' in 1 Timothy 3.1 and the word 'bishop' in the next verse is the same Greek word. How does Wright explain why he translated the two words differently?

20. In the context of his translation of 1 Timothy 2.12, how does the author explain why he uses male pronouns in 1 Timothy 3.1–7?

21. How does Wright explain the requirement that a bishop be the 'husband of one wife'?

22. In order to make the best use of time, consider creating a list of the requirements for bishop as well as for deacon prior to this session using the passage and Wright's explanation of their application. Note that he asserts that the requirements challenge the 'normal cultural expectations of male behaviour'.

23. 1 Timothy 3.14–16 quotes an early Christian hymn or prayer written to illuminate the 'mystery of Godliness'. When 1 Timothy was written the term 'mystery' meant something like the meaning of the word 'key' today, a concept which, when used in the right way, explains something you can see for yourself, but in fuller ways. There were 'mystery religions' in that day, in which an adherent was given additional information, insight or tools which might be used to gain understanding or a more powerful practice of the religion. There are still some organizations using similar strategies in our day. 'Mystery' did not mean 'unknowable' in Paul's time, as it does today. The 'mystery of godliness' is the story of Jesus.

Applying the Scriptures (15 minutes)

The purpose of this section of the study is to gather the threads discovered in the study and to weave them into a deeper understanding of the message of 1 Timothy. Use the suggested activities as time permits to extend what you have learned.

1. Compare and contrast the meanings and usages of these offices of the church: apostle, disciple, bishop, deacon and pastor.

2. Using the materials available, create a visual explanation of the relationship between the context of scripture when it was written down and its context today with reference to human behaviours. For example, what is the difference between stealing a coin in biblical times and stealing (cutting and pasting) intellectual property today? What difference does it make how long a person's hair is? Which translation or version of the Bible is the 'correct/best' among all of them? Why do we have so many of them anyway?

3. On page 15, the author writes, 'As so often in the New Testament, the call to prayer is also the call to think: to think clearly about God and the world, and God's project for the whole human race'. What examples of Christian thinking can you recall from this study, and how does one develop and practice this form of Christian discipline?

Sharing 'Oh Wow' Moments (5 minutes)

In these brief moments, members of the group can share moments of realization or reflection they experienced during this study.

Closing Prayer (1 minute)

God of all, help us to become deeper students of your word and more active doers of its message in the world. Grant us the grace of growing in maturity as we learn to live in Christian community. Amen.

Ticket Out the Door (3 minutes)

On the slip of paper provided, list one thing you learned well this session and one thing you want to understand better.

SESSION TWO: 1 TIMOTHY 4.1—6.21
INSTRUCTIONS FOR CHURCH LEADERS

(Pages 30–57)

Opening Prayer (1 minute)

Accept, noble Jesus, our gratitude for all you have done, are doing and will do in the life of your followers and their churches. We specifically thank you for your instruction in how to be the church, for your plan for us opposes so much of what our world teaches is valuable. Reset our default settings and restore us to a right relationship with you. Amen.

Group Opening (5 minutes)

From the responses at the end of the first session, choose several for discussion, using them to remind the group about the themes and points of emphasis in 1 Timothy.

Exploring the Scriptures (30 minutes)

1. N. T. Wright maintains it is false teaching to regard anything created by God as bad within itself rather than believing 'that the God who made the world in the first place is remaking it through Jesus and the spirit, and that we are called, not to abandon our humanity but to celebrate its rescue, redemption and remaking'.
2. How is thanksgiving, in Wright's words, the fundamental human and Christian stance on our relationship with the created world?
3. In 1 Timothy 4.6–10, Paul compares training for athletic competitions and training for spiritual growth as a Christian. Probably he meant that the goal of Christian life to become fully human, both maturing and mature, encompasses both physical and spiritual hard work. How does Wright apply this teaching to the work of Christian leaders?
4. How does Wright explain the three most common interpretations of 1 Timothy 4.10?
5. 'Give attention to reading', Paul tells Timothy in 1 Timothy 4.13. Why is close and prayerful reading such hard work, and what are the benefits of this command?
6. These instructions were written especially for Timothy, who served as a pastor, and are certainly appropriate for clergy in any circumstance. Perhaps it is not stretching the point to apply these encouragements to yourself as well. At the heart of this passage, Wright says, is the command 'pay attention to yourself'. What kind of person are you becoming?
7. As you read 1 Timothy 5.1–8, try to keep in mind the description of the Jerusalem church in Acts 2.43–47. Reread that passage from Acts as a refresher on what kind of life the leaders of the earliest churches envisioned for believers. At a minimum, it means that members in a local church would provide material and financial help for those in need. Widows were particularly vulnerable in those times since the roles allowed for women tended to be restrictive as well as not well remunerated.
8. How would Wright answer the charge that churches should be spiritual entities and not concerned with the physical needs of

people? How do the words 'power, sex and money' present a clue to the background of this passage?

9. What were the four obvious problems associated with widows in the church at Ephesus? What were Paul's answers to these challenges?

10. The instructions contained in 1 Timothy 5.17–25 are directed to churches concerning elders, in Greek called 'presbyters'. The initial instruction is that those elders who are good leaders and who work hard preaching and teaching are to be paid double. The second instruction seems intended to protect an elder from unwarranted accusations of wrongdoing.

11. In verse 21, the instructions are directed to elders themselves regarding discrimination on one hand against some persons and favouritism towards others on the other. Neither is acceptable. The best case, according to Paul, is to exercise extreme care in the ordination of candidates.

12. Wright imagines the world a thousand years from now and wonders what issues in the current church would most likely shock people then. He mentions sexual morality, the destruction of the created world through use of fossil fuels, racism, economic imperialism and slavery, whether as chattel or virtual slavery, i.e. 'wage slavery'. If we imagine the same thought experiment in the opposite direction, we might well identify the New Testament attitude towards slavery as the most shocking feature of that time. Wright points out that to be antislavery in Paul's day would be analogous to regarding cars, planes, trains and ships as unchristian in character. Wright continues by noting the position taken by New Testament writers that slave and master are equal before God and to treat each as having individual responsibility before God for his own behaviour. Paul seemed anxious also that Christians should avoid the reputation of disruptive or provocative behaviour, thereby establishing the conservative Christian standard for social change now common among churches.

13. Some things just don't change. Reading Paul's description in 6.3–5, one can imagine the faction seemingly in every church, never satisfied with anything and always grumbling about something. The great danger is that trust is broken, love disappears into contention and another church community crumbles in defeat. The New Testament is fearless in portraying church life as it really is. The answer to church dysfunction is given in the next passage for study.

14. Paul says that the answer to our question is godliness and contentment. 'If we have food and clothing', he says in 1 Timothy 6.8, 'we should be satisfied with it'. Are we capable of that discipline?

15. Wright identifies our problem explicitly on page 50: 'And yet every advertisement, every other television program, many movies and most political manifestos are designed, by subtle and not-so-subtle ways, to make us say, "If only I had just a bit more money, then I would be content"'.

16. How would you explain to a non-Christian the famous maxim in 1 Timothy 6.10: 'the love of money . . . is the root of all evil'? Wright continues, 'Money itself is not evil; but as verse 10 famously puts it, loving money is not only evil, it's the root of all evils' (page 51).

17. Wright asks what you would do if you found yourself confronting something that really frightened you, like a rhinoceros or a large spider. Of course, you would run away, just as he challenges the reader of 1 Timothy 6.11–16 to run away from the love of money or greed. Instead, chase after the list of desirable virtues listed next. 'Fight the noble fight of the faith', Paul encourages. Did you notice the intensity of the responses he commands? What other words could you choose to illuminate the urgency of your response to the sins Paul previously identified? How seriously did Paul imply that only a whole-hearted, muscular response would be sufficient against the temptations of greed?

18. Explain to a neighbour or to the whole group why the notion of 'epiphany' was a challenge to Roman rule. Why did Wright translate 'epiphany' as 'royal appearing'?

19. Why does Wright say that persons do not have an immortal soul? Which group of people was Paul countering with his teaching in this passage? How does Wright explain the life to come in human experience?

20. What noble profession did Jesus make before Pontius Pilate? What noble public profession do we make in claiming to be Christian, as in 1 Timothy 6.12?

21. At the end of his explanation of this passage, Wright describes the Christian response to greed, saying that a person who chases after the virtues listed in verse 11, who has worked to acquire and grow in those virtues, and who has chosen again and again to live the life asserted by Paul as Christian and to reject the traits valued by the world, is beginning to live in the present the life of the coming age (verse 12). That's the kind of person, Wright says in agreement with Paul, who will be ready for the royal appearing of Jesus.

22. In 1 Timothy 6.17–21, Paul highlights the difference between God and worldly riches. God's riches are always available to the believer, but the world's riches are too uncertain to set one's hopes on. Paul says that the rich in this world are to 'do good, to be rich in good works, generous and eager to share'. They can lay a deep foundation for the life of the age to come and gain real life in Christ.

23. Some persons are born poor; some persons are born into a rich family. Either way, Paul seems to be saying that each person is responsible for acting in a way consistent with the model of Jesus.

24. This letter ends with a warning against the dangers of 'knowledge'. Refer to the early discussion of mystery religions and the role of false teaching in how 'mysteries' were revealed to and used by the adherents of some religions during Paul's time. Wright notes that the Greek word for knowledge is *gnosis*, which lends its name to Gnosticism, a religion and philosophy which exists in some form still today. What were the main tenets of Gnosticism, and how was it a threat to early Christianity?

Applying the Scriptures (15 minutes)

The purpose of this section of the study is to gather the threads discovered in the study and to weave them into a deeper understanding of the message of 1 Timothy. Use the suggested activities as time permits to extend what you have learned.

1. If you created the chart on the roles of officers of the church in the previous session, update it now to include these roles: elder and widows.

2. Identify the major themes of 1 Timothy, such as sound doctrine, church leadership, spiritual training and the church as social caretaker. Create a visual explanation of the relationships between those themes in a format such as a Venn diagram, causal graph or tree diagram, or in any other way which is understandable to you and your group. Be prepared to present your findings.

3. Make a 'Top Ten' list of the most important verses or passages in 1 Timothy.

4. What are some common sayings you remember your grandparents or elders saying which counter the notion that 'greed is good'. Share those sayings with each other and the group.

Sharing 'Oh Wow' Moments (5 minutes)

In these brief moments, members of the group can share moments of realization or reproof they experienced during this study.

Closing Prayer (1 minute)

Gracious God, it is stunning to realize how far away we are from living your life for us today. Our culture seems fractured, bickering is too often the order of the day, and the voices of materialism drown out your voice of service and compassion for others. Give us the wisdom and determination to start anew today to model Christian life in our lives, and forgive us when we fail. Amen.

Ticket Out the Door (3 minutes)

Using a slip of paper, write down one thing you know about 2 Timothy and one thing you would like to learn about it. Give your response to the facilitator as you leave.

SESSION THREE: 2 TIMOTHY 1.1—4.22
POWER, LOVE AND SELF-CONTROL IN SERVICE

(Pages 61–97)

Opening Prayer (1 minute)

In your grace, royal Leader, we encounter the vigorous and truthful words of your servant Paul, who warns us of persecution to come in our lives and of strife for the sake of the gospel message of Jesus, and yet paints such a wondrous image of life in Christ that we willingly give our lives so that we can experience it. Where we fall short, forgive and help us to amend our lives, for your sake. Amen.

Group Opening (5 minutes)

From the responses at the end of the second session, choose several to respond to, using them to teach the group about the themes and points of emphasis in 2 Timothy.

Exploring the Scriptures (30 minutes)

1. From several passages in Paul's letters, we come away with the sense that Timothy was young and perhaps shy or anxious about taking a leadership role in the church. In 2 Timothy 1.1–7 Paul seems to be giving Timothy a 'pep talk' about stepping into that role with the confidence of knowing that he had been called to that ministry. Some commentators believe that this letter may have been the last written by Paul and was written with the expectation that he would

not live many years longer. In fact, 2 Timothy does follow loosely the pattern in Greek writing for a 'last will and testament' format.

2. Wright takes the three gifts of the spirit for leaders in order as in verse 7, beginning with power. He points out that leadership with power and responsibility is necessary to regulate the common life of a complex society. How would your definition of 'power' differ with reference to political leaders and religious leaders?

3. He then moves on to the next gift: love. How does Wright explain the role of love in effective religious leadership?

4. The author translates the next term as 'prudence', meaning something like wisdom set into meaningful action. Other translators choose 'self-discipline' or 'self-control', but all connote power held in reserve and used judiciously.

5. What does Wright tell us about the relationship between Paul and Timothy? What role does prayer play in their relationship and in the substance of this letter?

6. On page 65, what does Wright identify as the main theme of 2 Timothy 1.8–14?

7. In the commentary on verse 9, how does the author clarify the meaning of 'calling'? How does that sense of calling motivate the believer and determine the goals sought by the believer?

8. Wright offers three possible meanings for Paul's statement that 'everyone in Asia has turned away from me'. What were those three possibilities, and how do you evaluate them?

9. Who was Onesiphorus, and how did he serve Paul in 'severely practical ways'?

10. What was the 'work' described in 2 Timothy 2.1–7, and what images does Paul use for illustrating to Timothy the kind of work that he would be doing?

11. How was Paul's message about Jesus being risen from the dead and true Lord of the world offensive? How do Isaiah 40:6–8 and 55.10–11 relate to the passage in 2 Timothy?

12. On pages 74–75, Wright says of Paul: 'He does it (as he says in 2 Corinthians 4.7–15) for the sake of all God's people. It is as though he is drawing the enemy fire on to himself, to create a breathing space in which the young church can grow and develop, can become strong in faith and hope'. What heroic act of Paul's does Wright describe with these words?

13. Paul speaks of 'eternal glory' in verse 10. 'Glory' in the Old Testament usually referred to the blazing presence of God, but Wright connects eternal glory to what activity in eternity? What is the role of the faithful to be in eternity?

14. 'Warn them, in God's presence, not to quarrel about words', Paul writes in 2 Timothy 2.14. Some professions, like lawyers, politicians, preachers and teachers, thrive on discussing and arguing about words and their meanings. Even though you may not be tempted to engage in that particular exercise, some people feel compelled to argue with great passion about issues too small for others to notice. In this case, Paul refers to two men in verse 18 of this passage who are teaching that the resurrection has already happened. This problem, Paul says, will spread like a cancer. Using references like Colossians 3.1–4, false teachers suggested that the bodily resurrection was a crude and unnecessary way of presenting the sublime spiritual truth that faith is a spiritual experience in the present that leads to a disembodied eternal bliss.

15. To contrast a bad example of faithful Christian service, Paul presents a rock-solid servant of Jesus Christ: competent, experienced, effective in communication and thoroughly prepared to teach others the mysteries and wonders of the Christian faith. God bless all those who serve us with such nobility!

16. Returning to his theme of proper Christian behaviour, Paul gives two examples in 2 Timothy 2.20–26 of ways in which people dishonour themselves. Using Jesus as the model for service, Paul speaks directly to Timothy, giving him three ways to emulate Jesus. What are those three directives from Paul to Timothy?

17. Alan Jones, a pastor and theologian of an earlier day, wrote a book on the realities of Christian vocational service entitled *Sacrifice and Delight* (New York: HarperCollins, 1992) in which he described Christian ministry as occurring in the 'mean time' which would usually be interpreted to be between the resurrection and the royal appearing of Jesus. Jones, however, had in mind the situation described by Paul in 2 Timothy 3.1–9, with its shocking list of people's behaviours. Wright suggests that rather than focusing on the behaviours themselves, the reader should consider the effects those behaviours have on those who engage in them as well as the effects they have on those whose lives are touched by such people. What response does he make to answer these questions?

18. Paul next turns to the problem of those whose false teaching is so full of the sense of proper faith that they can persuade, cajole or bully the more vulnerable and less sure to adopt beliefs not in line with the message of Jesus. Jannes and Jambres, two persons from Exodus 7, are presented as exemplars of this sort of false teaching. How did Paul apply their story to this instance?

19. The author tells the story of a visiting professor and his wife exploring the older parts of the college at the university where the

professor would be teaching. What use did Wright make of that story, and how did he apply it to 2 Timothy 3.10–17?

20. Wright describes the meaning of the word 'inspired' and explores three ways the word 'inspired' is used today. Clarify what that means by creating a list of Wright's responses and discussing the meaning of those responses. Wright encourages us to affirm that the spirit who caused the scriptures to be written, who spoke through the different writers in so many ways, is as powerful today as ever, and that power, through the written word, can transform lives. Wright asserts on page 88 that 'scripture not only gives us true information about how our lives can be transformed; it will itself be a part of that process'.

21. Imagine a sports team facing the final minutes of a contest, behind in the score but only by a margin that can be overcome if a combination of concentration, exhaustive effort and good luck provides the opportunity. Some teams might be content to play out the game and congratulate the winning team. Some teams might decide that if they can't win, they can at least punish the other team by committing unnecessary fouls. Some few teams will focus their own talents, skills and effort to the attempt to overcome the opponent and win the contest. In 2 Timothy 4.1–5, Paul seems to be encouraging Timothy to 'get on with his work' and win the day. Verse 2 explains how that can be done: announce the message; keep going and rebuke, warn and encourage all with patience and explanation. Young teachers, and young professionals in any job, find this last part of verse 2 particularly difficult. The tendency to state the case aggressively and to blame the class when it does not perform seems to offer a safer alternative than dealing with difficult individuals and stubborn factions. The resulting stalemate is the subject of verses 3 and 4. Paul exhorts Timothy to keep going and to keep his balance, to keep his head.

22. Paul could likely remember when he was in a similar situation to Timothy's and how difficult it was to keep working with no goal in sight. In 2 Timothy 4.6–8, Paul uses four overlapping pictures to depict the goal ahead of Timothy. Make a list of the four images and the particular lesson each picture teaches.

23. Identify each person mentioned in 2 Timothy 4.9–22 and note the significance of each one.

Applying the Scriptures (15 minutes)

The purpose of this section of the study is to gather the threads discovered in the study and to weave them into a deeper understanding of the message of 2 Timothy. Use the suggested activities as time permits to extend what you have learned.

1. Paul used the example of a workman as a worthy model for Christian pastors and teachers. To extend that image for our time, a competent sewer, woodworker, machinist or quilter may more readily come to mind. Reread the description in 2 Timothy 2.15 and recall the person who came to your mind as you read. Share that person's story, if you know it, and why you feel that person is a good example of the ideal presented in this scripture.

2. Second Timothy 3.17 says that the purpose of the scriptures is 'so that people who belong to God may be complete, fitted out and ready for every good work'. Wright says, 'The aim is (verse 17) not to squash people into a strange, unnatural shape by trying to order their lives according to the Bible, but to help people who belong to God to become complete, richly human beings, reflecting God's image in all its many-sided splendor'. St. Francis might be one good example of such a person. Have you encountered other examples in history or in your own life? Share with the group their inspirational stories.

3. What words do you recall from 2 Timothy which seem to characterize the message of this letter? Create a visual representation of your findings and present them to the group.

Sharing 'Oh Wow' Moments (5 minutes)

In these brief moments, members of the group can share moments of realization or reproof they experienced during this study.

Closing Prayer (1 minute)

We thank you, Lord, for the lives of Timothy, Eunice and Lois, for Paul and Onesiphorus, whose dedication to you motivates us to follow their examples and to live lives of devotion to you and service to others. Amen.

Ticket Out the Door (3 minutes)

On a piece of paper, make two predictions about the teachings in the letter to Titus.

SESSION FOUR: TITUS 1.1–3.15
BUILT ON JESUS CHRIST

(Pages 99–119)

Opening Prayer (1 minute)

Jesus, we ask in your name that our study will be profitable to you, your people and your church. Open our hearts and fill them with love for others, open our minds to imagine the directions our lives and our ministries may take and remake our wills to live as you command rather than in the values of the world. Amen.

Group Opening (5 minutes)

From the responses at the end of the third session, choose several to respond to, using them to teach the group about the themes and points of emphasis in Titus.

Exploring the Scriptures (15 minutes)

1. What is the 'two ages' schema for understanding the history taught by Jews and adapted by Paul for the Christian church? In which age did Christian believers live? How does 1 Corinthians 13.11 fit into this schema?
2. Some people living in Paul's time and in modern times misunderstand the dangers of polytheism, thinking 'How great, a god for every need', instead of 'Which of these gods can I really trust?' Protection from the gods was at least as important as belief because how would one know if, in serving one god, another had been offended?
3. What do we know about Titus and his relationship with Paul?
4. What life experience does the author relate to the need for structure in the early church?
5. Titus 1.5–9 contains Paul's instructions to Titus concerning his responsibilities in Crete as well as the traits required for appointment as elder/presbyter/bishop. What are these characteristics? Restate these in your own terms and understanding.
6. Wright says, 'The fashionable stance in today's Western world is against strong, clear teaching'. On the other hand, all of the Pastoral Letters warn against the temptations in following false teachers. Could false teachers be strong, clear teachers as well as wrong?
7. In Titus 1.10–16, Paul tells Titus to be wary of those in Crete who seem to be preaching the necessity of following Jewish law, especially circumcision, as a prerequisite for Christian living. What has

come from that practice that is dangerous to Christians, according to Paul?

8. Describe the 'young philosophers puzzle' Wright introduces in this passage. How does Paul use a form of it to describe the Cretans?

9. The Cretans insist on following Jewish law. What paradox does this create in their own moral state, as clarified by Wright on page 107?

10. Wright summarizes the message of Titus 2.1–10 on page 112. Restate that message for a neighbour.

11. Titus 2.11–15 contains Paul's instructions for Christians living in the hope of the royal appearing of Jesus the king. Ask someone in the group to describe how Wright clarifies the meaning of those instructions.

12. Verse 14 of this passage commends 'good works' as a task for God's people. In 3.1, 3.8 and 3.14 this action is commanded for believers. What does Wright think that Paul means by 'good works'?

13. Paul talks about the 'new birth' in Titus 3.1–8a, which is discussed in the third chapter of John's gospel but hardly occurs at all in other Christian writings. Wright connects 'new birth' to 'washing' and then to 'baptism'. What scripture references does Wright introduce in support, and in reference to 1 Corinthians 12. How does he extend this message further?

14. On page 116, Wright emphasizes the connection between the sacrificial gift of salvation in Jesus Christ and the character of his followers by stating: 'What we see, in a life transformed by the gospel, is the direct result of God's lavish, generous love. *And that's why he wants us to be generous, kind and gentle in turn*'. Apply this teaching to your own life, and reflect on the actions you need to take to bring your life into compliance with this directive.

15. Paul's final advice to Titus regarding those determined to pursue teaching that is not in accord with the message of Jesus is found in Titus 3.10–11. 'If someone is causing divisions, give them a first warning, then a second, and then avoid them. You know a person like that is twisted, sinful and self-condemned.' How would you reconcile this advice with the command to be 'gentle' in our actions?

Applying the Scriptures (30 minutes)

The purpose of this section of the study is to gather the threads discovered in the study and to weave them into a deeper understanding of the message of Titus as well as summarizing activities for *1 and 2 Timothy and Titus for Everyone*. Use the suggested activities as time permits to extend what you have learned.

1. On page 118, Wright observes that 'Titus is to set up what we today would call a charity organization.' The author continues with an explanation for that observation, the motivation for that behaviour, and a reference to Jesus' command to do so. How is this charity-mindedness related to Paul's teaching of 'good works'? Create a response in order to lead a group discussion on this topic.
2. Imagine that you have been given an assignment to write a blog on: 'How do you recognize false teaching today?' Using the current study, what would you say? You might either write the blog and share it with others or prepare an outline for the contents of the blog.
3. Paul states in several places in the Pastoral Letters that Christians are called to serve others, to spread the gospel message and to work in their churches for 'the age to come'. Yet far too many churches are primarily composed of inactive Christians who make little effort to live out their faith. If you were leading an effort in your church to motivate and involve these inactive Christians, what steps would you take? Use scripture and your study of this book as the basis for your recommendations.
4. With reference to the teachings of Paul, the guidance of N. T. Wright and your own life experience, what would an ideal church be like? This thought experiment is suggested to stimulate your own imagination and your own conscience about the manner in which you might contribute to this 'ideal' church. Fashion a response in any form which suits your gifts and your resources.

Sharing 'Oh Wow' Moments (5 minutes)

In these brief moments, members of the group can share moments of realization or reproof they experienced during this study.

Closing Prayer (1 minute)

We worship you for who you are, almighty God. We love you because you first loved us. We serve you in the model lived by our saviour, Jesus. We live so that others may know the love which emboldens and gladdens us. We pray for our leaders in the world and in our church that they may recognize and follow your guidance. We depart in the peace of your presence and in the grace to become what you will for us. Amen.

Ticket Out the Door (3 minutes)

Respond to this prompt: What great things happened in our study of *1 and 2 Timothy and Titus for Everyone*?

www.ingramcontent.com/pod-product-compliance
Lightning Source LLC
LaVergne TN
LVHW080510291224
800028LV00026BA/257